HAVE THIS MIND

HAVE THIS MIND

BY

GERALD KENNEDY

*"Have this mind in you, which was
also in Christ Jesus . . ."*

PHILIPPIANS 2:5

HARPER & BROTHERS PUBLISHERS

NEW YORK *and* LONDON

HAVE THIS MIND

Copyright, 1948, by Gerald Kennedy
Printed in the United States of America

All rights in this book are reserved.

FIRST EDITION

B-X

This is for Milton F. Steinford

PREFACE

Sermons ought to be preached and not written; they ought to be heard and not read. The style of the spoken word differs from the style of the written word. If any man has had his sermon taken down verbatim as he preached it, he knows that it must be edited before it is readable. After it has gone through that process, however, it is never quite the same. It never follows necessarily, therefore, that the preacher can write or the writer can preach.

This seems to me to be the main difficulty standing in the way of writing sermons. The path followed here has been a compromising one. That is, I have tried to keep some of the informality of the spoken word and yet not make it too unpleasant for those who expect a more formal prose style. The result, like most compromises, may not be too satisfactory to anyone.

The theme of the book is the great affirmations of the Christian Gospel, which when accepted, create the Christian mind. We preachers find ourselves being asked these days what Christians believe and in what ways they differ from non-Christians. Is a Christian a man who believes a certain creed, or is he a member of a certain organization, or is he one with a special spiritual experience? It seems to me that all of these things are helpful in defining a Christian. But essentially, we are Christians when our minds have accepted Jesus as our truth. A Christian is one who has the mind of Christ. These sermons are an attempt to enlarge on that idea and define that mind.

I write under the conviction that Christianity has the

only answer to the contemporary crisis. But I have the conviction also, that too many of us will never be the answer
to anything until we commit ourselves to Jesus Christ as
the truth. A young man said to me one night after a lecture,
"If Christians work so slowly and we have so little time,
what hope is there?" Only an awakening to the need for
the heroic acceptance of Christ's way can save us. Only
preaching with a terrible sense of urgency is of any avail
now.

I am grateful to my wife who spent many a long hour
trying to tighten my careless constructions. I am under
great obligations to my secretary, Miss Clarice Purdy, who
managed to get the manuscript ready in spite of an already
overcrowded schedule.

GERALD KENNEDY

CONTENTS

ACKNOWLEDGMENTS

The author wishes to express his appreciation to the following authors, agents and publishers for permission to quote from their copyrighted works:

Brandt & Brandt for "Thirty-five" from *The Last Circle* by Stephen Vincent Benét.

Abingdon-Cokesbury Press for "The Agony of God" from *The Glory of God* by Georgia Harkness.

Mrs. Bonaro W. Overstreet for "To One Who Doubts the Worth of Doing Anything If You Can't Do Everything."

HAVE THIS MIND

I

TRUTH FOR CHRISTIANS

> *". . . neither be ye of doubtful mind."*
>
> LUKE 12:29

Jesus went out of his way to warn his disciples and would-be disciples that they must expect conflict and danger. In the world there would be tribulation. He saw life in terms of crises, and even as the opposition arose against himself, he knew it would rise against his followers. We shall not feel sorry for ourselves or deceived, therefore, if we are confronted with hatred and bitterness. Always there is the World against the Church, and Evil against Goodness. Our life is not an easy thing, and so far as we can tell, it never will be.

But the serious thing for the Christian is the controversy and conflict within himself. It is then that the Gospel becomes not peace but a sword. There is probably no unhappier man in the world than the Christian with a doubtful mind. He tries to justify hatred in time of war, but he remembers that Jesus said: "Love your enemies." He makes excuses for his sharp business practices, but he remembers the command: "Give to him that asketh." He hears the call to sacrificial living, but he is still enamored with the idea of comfort.

Hatred and prejudice on the part of people who do not know any better are tragic yet understandable. But what shall we say about such attitudes from the person who has accepted the Christian heritage and has even said yes to it publicly? How can he justify his refusal to practice brotherhood? Or what about the Christian who is entirely

1

relativistic in his decisions? In one instance he may react according to the New Testament ethic, but in another case, where there is more at stake financially, he may decide to deny the New Testament teaching.

This is the great failure of the Church. It is full of people who are not committed to the proposition that Jesus was truth. We have said yes outwardly but inwardly we hold many reservations. Each decision causes a debate between what Christ said and what we want. We made a choice, but are afraid of its implications. We follow too many leaders and worship too many idols. Nothing has been decided, and we are in a constant state of misery. This game we play of matching our selfish wills against our Lord's, seems to be clever but it is not satisfying. Jesus said, "Neither be ye of doubtful mind."

It is this continual uncertainty as to what Christians will do under pressure that weakens our whole mission. Except in the relatively unimportant matters, we seldom give a unified impression. In our desire to make our doctrines acceptable to worldlings, we have minimized the positive words of the Gospel. But this has not worked in making the Gospel either effective or acceptable. Paul was speaking to this situation when he said, "Have this mind in you, which was also in Christ Jesus" (Philippians 2:5). Ah, that's it. The solution lies in having our minds transformed into the likeness of Christ's. We have to look at life through his eyes and think of human experience as he thought of it. Christian actions can spring only from Christian motives. We must begin thinking within the framework of the mind of Christ.

What Is Christianity?

Once again we need to look at this religion of ours and ask ourselves what it is. What think we of Christ and the Christian way? There has always been a conflict between

those who would make Christianity entirely a matter of
supernatural revelation and those who would make it
merely down to earth common sense. That is, some Christian thinkers have felt that our Faith came through a
special revelation of God only, and it has nothing whatever
to do with logic or intellectual investigation. Tertullian, in
a treatise written about A.D. 200 on "The Wisdom of This
World," stated the position in these words:

> What is there in common between Athens and Jerusalem?
> What between the Academy and the Church? What between
> heretics and Christians? . . . Away with all projects for a "Stoic"
> a "Platonic" or a "dialectic" Christianity! After Christ Jesus
> we desire no subtle theories, no acute enquiries after the
> gospel . . .

The other extreme has been a more popular view in our
time, and it is often associated with the study of compara-
tive religions. Christianity is here regarded as simply one
religion among many without very much in it that is unique.
Of course, that there is good and truth in all religions, this
viewpoint would agree. But none of them is regarded as
having a monopoly on truth, and in general, one is felt
to be about as good as another. At least, this position would
maintain that there is no sense in getting excited about
converting people from another religion to Christianity.

This conflict came out at the Madras Missionary Conference. Dr. Hendrik Kraemer had prepared a statement on
"The Christian Message in a Non-Christian World." He
insisted that Judaism and Christianity are what he called
"revelational," and all other religions are "rationalistic."
This, the Conference would not accept. Finally, a committee, of which Dr. Kraemer was a member, drew up a statement which seems to me nearer the truth than either
extreme. Among other things, the committee said this:

> There are many non-Christian religions that claim the al-
> legiance of multitudes. We see and readily recognize that in

them are to be found values of deep religious experience, and great moral achievements. Yet we are bold enough to call men out from them to the feet of Christ. We do so because we believe that in Him alone is the full salvation which man needs.[1]

Not many Christians would believe that God has spoken only to a Semitic tribe at the east end of the Mediterranean Sea. But we deny our whole tradition if we do not believe that He spoke in a special way there and He bestows gifts on men through Christ, that they can receive from no other source.

A few years ago it was popular to urge the scientific approach to Christianity. We believed that the scientific spirit was the answer to all our problems, and too many Christian leaders assumed that the only way to save Christianity was to adjust it to this spirit. We watered down everything suggesting revelation and played up everything that could suggest objective experimentation. The results were not particularly happy.

We found all we had left after that process was an emasculated code of ethics without authority or urgency. To approach Christianity with the attitude of doubting every affirmation until it can be proved, will never make a man a Christian nor give him any power to live by. Christianity can be tried and tested. It must be judged by its fruits. But in the beginning there must be an act of faith by which God in Christ breaks into human consciousness like lightning. It is more like a miracle than an argument. The acceptance of the Christian revelation as truth is the beginning of a man's Christian adventure.

We must confess that Christianity is not attractive to the worldling. Who wants to accept the impossible ethics of the Sermon on the Mount? Who will say that he is willing to lose his life for Christ's sake, if he weighs this demand against his human desire for comfort and selfish advantage?

[1] Van Dusen, *World Christianity*, Abingdon-Cokesbury, 1947, 194.

What man in the control of white hot anger will seriously consider loving his enemy? None of this makes sense when it is approached from the standpoint of the wisdom of the world. On the contrary, it all looks like madness. How clearly Paul understood this. Remember Festus' word to him after his defense before Agrippa: "Paul, thou art mad; thy much learning is turning thee mad" (Acts 26:24). I wonder how many similar experiences lay back of Paul's word to the Corinthians:

> Seeing that Jews ask for signs, and Greeks seek after wisdom: but we preach Christ crucified, unto Jews a stumblingblock, and unto Gentiles foolishness. I CORINTHIANS 1:22-23.

The demands of the Gospel make sense only to the man whose worldly carefulness has been washed away. First must come the plunge. First there must be the acquiescence of faith. First a man must say that he will take the Christian truth for his truth and be obedient to it. Only then will the foolishness seem to be wisdom, and the wisdom of the world appear to be foolishness. Only then will a Christian stop asking for a sign and be content with the inner assurance of the Gospel.

The demand of Christianity is never partial, but totalitarian. It is a revelation of Truth, not truths. We are tempted to say we will accept part of it for limited areas of our lives. We want to say, "This far, but no farther." It is in vain. A Catholic layman said one time that if you cut the little finger of the Catholic Church, it bleeds to death. However that may be, if you cut off a small part of Christian truth it bleeds to death. Its vitality is in its wholeness.

Christians in all probability will never be in the majority. The world's glittering foolishness will always appeal to more people than Christ's truth. But the mere fact of majority on the other side becomes less and less important. Christians are not people who get their opinions from a

Gallup Poll. The majority can be wrong, and often the
majority is wrong. The Christian says, "No matter what the
multitude is shouting, what does Christ say? If I cannot
have his word of approval, all the shouting means nothing."

> Like Verdi, when at his worst opera's end
> The mad houseful's plaudits near outbang his
>   orchestra,
> He looks through all the roaring and the wreaths
> Where sits Rossini silent in his stall . . .
> One wise man's verdict outweighs all the fools.[2]

The Continental theologians have a phrase I like. They
say that Christianity is a "confessional faith." They mean a
man is not and cannot be automatically a Christian. We
once had the idea that it would be possible to make Christians out of our children without their knowing what had
happened to them. No, that is a vain hope precisely because a confessional faith demands a personal confession.
Somewhere we must say that we accept it as our truth. No
matter how pious our homes or our environment, still, the
Gospel will not be satisfied with less than our personal
declaration of purpose. Every Christian has to know he is
a Christian because he has confessed its truth.

The Authority of Christianity

A narrow dogmatism so often associated with authoritative Christianity, is one of the most distasteful things to en-
counter. It only appeals to a certain type of mind which
manifests itself in other activities besides religion. You see
it in the political reactionaries and in the rugged individ-
ualists. You find it in men who hope that their antisocial
practices may yet turn back the clock. It is present in
racketeers. When such as these become Christians, they are
often narrow and prejudiced in that area too. I dread to

[2] Quoted by Zeller, *Peace Is Our Business,* House of the Church of
the Brethren, 1947, 90.

see one of my young people marry a person with a religion of this type, for I fear that such a person will show that same spirit in all his relationships. Narrow dogmatists are not lovable people. They are not nice to have around too much nor too near.

The authority of Christianity is that terrible kind of authority without external compulsion. Being free is not living without restraint nor doing just what we please. It is living in harmony with what we are and obeying the deep demands of our being. It is belonging to a beloved community and bearing one's share of its responsibilties. Any other kind of freedom is license, which one day becomes the worst slavery of all.

The miraculous thing about the authority of Christianity is its sense of release. The ship with the broken rudder is in a sense freer than the one under the control of the helmsman. But as it veers with every wind and threatens to turn over with every sudden squall, it is a travesty on the concept of freedom. The ship is running free when it is fulfilling its destiny, which is to say, the purpose for which it was created. So, the straight and narrow path of the Christian comes to be a roomier place than the wide way which leads to destruction.

The mistake we have made is our assumption that either men must be anarchists or fascists. This is as foolish as insisting that a man must either remain single or have a harem, as Chesterton once put it. The essential point is where the authority comes from and whether or not we accept it from within. Life without order is intolerable. Life with rules enforced by men we do not respect is intolerable. Life is satisfactory only when we have found the real authority which can neither be escaped nor denied. To seek compromise with that authority is personal destruction.

This is the authority of Jesus. We do not make enough

of his ability to command men. Consider this characteristic in his own lifetime. The wonder is not that men crucified him, for we are always killing the best we know and destroying the thing we love. But the wonder is that men could not forget Jesus. Even when they denied him, they could not forget him. Even when they derided him as a fool, they remembered what he said. His was the authority of their own hearts and their own deep longings. His was the authority of the way things·are. And his Gospel is the authority of truth. Jesus was right!

This authority of Christ cannot be forced on people who have not accepted his way. Young people brought up in the loose sexual thinking of the time will not regard their bodies as temples of the Holy Spirit until they have freely accepted Christ. Businessmen without the mind of Christ will regard Christian ethics in business as silly. Authority by force is no authority at all and only reveals an inner weakness. Iron curtains and secret police are not signs of strength, but of fear. When the Church has attempted that kind of enforcement in the name of Christ, it has betrayed him.

His is always a personal authority. Truth about facts is useful and important. But back of that, there is the truth of interpretation. What do they mean? When we find that, we are in the presence of personal truth, and for men, that is ultimate. It is here we move into the realm of meaning. Because the Christian interpretation of things makes sense by accounting for life as a whole, it is the only satisfying and convincing truth.

Emerson was aware of this character of the Gospel and of our failure to let it fulfill this function through us when he wrote of a certain preacher

> who sorely tempted me to say I would go to church no more. A snowstorm was falling around us. The snowstorm was real; the preacher merely spectral, and the eye felt the sad contrast in

looking at him, and then out of the window behind him, into the beautiful meteor of the snow. He had lived in vain. He had not one word intimating that he had laughed or wept, was married or in love, had been commended, or cheated, or chagrined. If he had ever lived and acted, we were none the wiser for it. The capital secret of his profession, namely, to convert life into truth, he had not learned.

It is this power of converting life into truth which Jesus had, that turns his words into authoritative demands.

Too many of us are not yet convinced of the realism of Jesus. We still want to think of him as a dreaming idealist who said many nice things which are pleasant to repeat. But we are of doubtful mind when it comes to taking the Christian way as the realistic way. We do not believe that Jesus' words are descriptions of the way things are. We regard them as mere poetic fantasies. Then like Emerson's preacher, we have about us an air of pious unreality.

His authority possesses men like a vision of the real. For the first time we know that we are seeing truth. The doubting which has kept us from achievement is taken away. The desire to roam every inviting bypath no longer haunts us. The regret we felt because there was so much to give up, leaves us. Doubts are gone and at last we live under the same discipline that guides the stars. We are going where we want to go.

A generation that fled from the authority of religion, turns in desperation to magic. A British organization conducted a survey recently to determine how many people still have the habit of prayer. It was discovered that about half the population of England still prays either regularly or occasionally. But the number who have maintained the habit of prayer is much lower than the number—nearly seven out of ten—who follow a superstitious ritual like throwing spilled salt over the shoulder. Whenever men flee from the authority of truth, they finally end up captive in the prison of superstition.

The Demand for Risk

The Christian Gospel, having claimed the truth of God as its foundation, does not hesitate to demand risk in the name of that truth. How cleverly we have covered over this part of the Gospel. After we assumed that comfort meant progress, and ease was synonomous with goodness, we were prepared to eliminate risk from Christianity. It is alarming to note the number of Christians who insist that no one can expect them to make a Christian decision if it will cost them anything. Too many men in business are sure that if it is a common practice, that is reason enough for them to follow it, though it may be utterly pagan in its consequences. Who could be expected to vote for an unrestricted neighborhood if it would lower property values, they want to know.

It is not true that the mere announcement of Christian principles will effect much in a society. The Gospel demands response because its truth is made manifest in personal action and personal relationships. Christian truth must be activated and often the action is in the realm of the unprovable. This demand for action is often overlooked by a philosophically-minded generation. It is amazing how many Christians have come to assume that their faith is only a matter of meditation and contemplation. Against this tendency, Kierkegaard rebelled with bitterness, and he was right. He pointed out time after time that the Christian is confronted with a demand for a choice, a decision, an action. This is the chief difference between a religion and a philosophy.

Here is the whole point of Jesus' parable of the house on the sand and the house on the rock. The contrast between the two types of people described is not that of mockers over against the pious. It is not sinner against saint. It is not the lost as opposed to the saved. It is the difference between a man who listens to the teaching and does nothing about it, and the man who obeys through actions patterned after Jesus' commands.

Carlyle's description of Cromwell could well be the New Testament description of the true disciple:

> Perhaps of all the persons in that anti-Puritan struggle, from first to last, the single indispensable one was Cromwell. To see, and dare, and decide, to be a fixed pillar in a welter of uncertainty: a king among men whether they called him so or not.

To find men like that was more important than to have geniuses as disciples. Jesus seems to have assumed that if he could find a dozen or so peasants who would let themselves be saturated with his truth, and then hold to it with tenacity and a single mind, he could build on that foundation. They were not supermen. But their faith in him made them strong enough to witness against the falsity of the world, even when it cost them their lives.

We who have adjusted our faith to our comfort are at a total loss when the crisis comes. It is then that we are revealed as mere Christian dilettantes, useless in the hour of trial. The tragedy is not only that of our cause, but it is the tragedy of individual failure. For then we know that because we have nothing we are willing to risk something for, we have nothing to live for. We have not been brave enough to find the truth.

The very nature of Christianity is exciting and if it is truly understood, it will have its real appeal to the daring. Only a deadening familiarity has hidden this true nature of our Faith. Its outreach is so great that the timid shrink from accepting its implications. Its horizon stretches too far for the careful and the prudent. Once its truth is accepted, everything is different. One has to rethink his attitudes and his aims. Commonplace things become miraculous signs of grace, and old things become new. But all of this, in the words of St. Paul, demands a willingness to become a fool for Christ's sake.

In March of 1860, the following advertisement appeared in the San Francisco papers:

> WANTED: Young skinny wiry fellows not over 18. Must be expert riders willing to risk death daily. Orphans preferred. Wages $25 per week. Apply Central Overland Express, Alta Bldg., Montgomery St.

A war makes the same demands and pays even less money, yet there is never a dearth of volunteers. Perhaps this is the truth about us after all. Perhaps we are not truly employed until we have accepted the hard sayings of our religion. Perhaps Jesus Christ is the savior of men, for one thing, because he does not hesitate to ask us for what seems to be impossible sacrifices.

The Christian Mind

A Russian boy was being tried for refusing to bear arms. Carefully he gave his reasons, showing that he had thought it all out clearly and had a reason for his opinions. The judge listened to the end and then he said impatiently, "Your position would be logical if the Kingdom of God had come. But it hasn't." Quickly the boy replied, "It has for me." This is the Christian's answer to all the so-called practical people who urge waiting until some more convenient season. The Devil's tempting word usually comes to say that the idea is a good one, but this is not the time for it. Here is an institution that has been practicing race discrimination for fifty years, and while it is unfortunate of course, still, the time has not yet arrived when the policy should be changed. Here is an instance of injustice in our community which is to be deplored, and someday, something ought to be done about it. But the time is not yet. This practice of mine is not in harmony with what I know to be the mind of Christ, and it should be eliminated. But not now! This is the height of denial, and it is our worst betrayal because it is the most cowardly.

Too many men live lives of apologetic negation. They find it necessary to cover up the things which they know are wrong. They find themselves seeking comfort by accepting the mediocre morality of the market place. They are driven to compare their compromising lives with those who are obviously inferior to them. They must protect themselves against the searching light of the Holy Spirit. Their prayers are perfunctory and ineffective because true prayer demands honesty and that is just the thing they cannot afford.

Such people become crowd people, for that is the only place they feel safe. They must protect their fearful hearts. Life that should be spontaneous and free becomes confined and haunted. They have dabbled in religion just enough to be troubled. Sometimes they go through life desperately unhappy, masking their real condition from all but their closest friends. Sometimes the strain becomes too much and they end up at the psychiatrist or perhaps in a mental hospital. They are the negative people, unable to reach the positive level.

Van Wyck Brooks said that, among the people he talked with, he noted a hunger for affirmations. There is a hunger in every man for affirmations. We are made to affirm and not to deny. We are created for positive, meaningful life, and not a furtive hiding of our secret selves from even our own consciousness. We need to find truth, for only then can we be unafraid and at liberty. It is love that can cast out our fear. To accept for ourselves the mind of Christ as our truth, is to learn love.

The mind of Christ leads us to God. Belief in God, which was so inevitable for Jesus and is so unescapable for the Christian, is often difficult for the irreligious man. It is not that one is more naïve than the other. It is rather that the Christian has had his eyes opened and his heart made

sensitive. He has had his mind illumined and God can speak
and be heard. For truth can never be convincing unless a
man has prepared his mind to receive it. Truth is kept out
by arrogance and fear. Truth enters when the mind has been
cleansed and made pure.

We are told sometimes that all we need do is practice
the golden rule. But this golden-rule religion is so often
ineffectual and comfortable. It is easy to make one's life a
benevolent neutrality in the name of the golden rule. For
it all depends on the kind of person who is practicing it.
The materialist may in all honesty do to others about what
he would like them to do for him, and do them a great
injury. The pagan may do unto others as he wants them to
do unto him, and desecrate a personality. The rule is of
value only when it is practiced within the framework of
the Christian mind. Let a man have the mind of Christ
and then practice the golden rule. But let us not begin to
do things for others until Christ has redeemed our minds.

The foundation stone of our faith is the affirmation that
God is like Jesus. This is so central that one would think
it could never be forgotten. But even theologians can forget
it. One of the most distressing things is to read a learned
volume on Christian thought by a profound scholar and
find that he has lost sight of this central truth. He wrestles
with all the problems of Deity, but he forgets the Christian
key to the solution of the difficulties. Paul said it perfectly:
"God was in Christ reconciling the world unto himself"
(II Corinthians 5:19).

The thought is too simple for us. We shrink from adjusting ourselves to this affirmation. We can believe that Jesus
taught some rather good things about God. We are willing
to declare that he knew God better than we know Him.
But to believe that in Jesus Christ we have the clue to
the mystery of God, is too direct and pointed. Yet, when

we speak of the mind of Christ, we mean the mind that revealed God.

The old phrase was "to accept Christ." What did that mean? Too often it meant to be willing that one's own shortcomings should be made up by Christ. It meant to let the Cross free us from any further responsibility and guilt. At its worst, it meant that we were willing to let Christ do whatever was necessary to save our poor, miserable souls after death. But to accept Christ means to take his truth for our own. It means to look at life and men through his eyes. It means to take his yoke upon us and bear it manfully. It means to wait patiently until he can impart the qualities of his mind to our minds. It means to confess his truth as our truth.

I do not know a better way to sum up this thought than to give you the words Dostoevski wrote to a woman who had befriended him in prison. He was describing his creed and he said:

> This credo is very simple. Here it is: to believe that there is nothing more beautiful, more profound, more sympathetic, more reasonable, more manly, and more perfect than Christ, and not only is there nothing, but, I tell myself with jealous love, there can be nothing. Besides, if anyone proved to me that Christ was outside the truth, and it really was so that the truth was outside Christ, then I should prefer to remain with Christ than with the truth.

Does this sound extreme? Perhaps it is. Yet how it shames our large pretensions and our small responses. What a difference there is between this testimony and the negative careful creeds. The truth for Christians is the mind of Christ. Once we have accepted that truth, it leads us to life.

II

IN THE BEGINNING

> *"I am the Alpha and the Omega, saith
> the Lord God, who is and who was
> and who is to come, the Almighty."*
> REVELATION 1:8

The Greek mathematician and inventor Archimedes
who lived in the third century B.C., once made a remark that
has been quoted ever since. Said he, "Give me a place to
stand and I will move the earth." We repeat those words
not because we expect to find a place from which we can
move the earth, at least not in the near future. But they
indicate one of the questions we have to make up our minds
about before we can live. Where shall we stand? Where
do we begin? Upon what foundation are we to build?

The starry-eyed dreamers and the self-conscious idealists
choose some utopia. But it is terribly difficult to stand on
something that has not yet materialized. The doubter
chooses skepticism until he discovers that it takes more
faith to believe in his doubts than it does to believe in
affirmations. He tries the impossible task of making a faith
out of his skepticism. The materialist chooses power and
takes his stand on the proposition that if enough power
can be developed and controlled by him, life will make
sense. Power, however, is shifting and unstable. Human
wisdom is never satisfactory as a foundation. It outruns its
controls and is corrupted by pride. None of these things
works. From them, nothing can be moved.

Now it has been characteristic of our time to regard God
as one possible place to stand, among several. We have as-

sumed we could take Him or leave Him. Belief in God, we have thought, was a free option. In spite of our failures to learn how to live together without Him, we cannot disenthrall ourselves from the idea that it ought to be possible to make human relations satisfactory without God. But Christianity's answer is simple and plain. A man must begin with God and build his structure on Him. Paul writes to the Corinthians: "According to the grace of God which was given unto me, as a wise masterbuilder I laid a foundation" (I Corinthians 3:10). To this demand of the Gospel there is no exception. Personal life has to be built on God. Social life cannot long endure without Him. All our international plans will never get past the dreaming stage, until we come to terms with God.

Jesus had to face this question of a beginning. It has been pointed out rightly that he said much more about human relations than he did about God. He was not an academic theologian. But we will miss the whole point if we do not see that, underneath all he said about men, there was a great affirmation about God. Remember how a man came to him one time and said:

> What commandment is the first of all? Jesus answered, The first is, Hear, O Israel; The Lord our God, the Lord is one: and thou shalt love the Lord thy God with all thy heart, and with all thy soul, and with all thy mind, and with all thy strength. The second is this, Thou shalt love thy neighbor as thyself. There is none other commandment greater than these. MARK 12:28-31.

Humanistic Christians have been so concerned in pointing out that Jesus made the second command important, they have overlooked the fact that he made it a second command. In other words, Jesus agreed with the Book of Exodus in making the first command, loyalty and obedience to God.

The tragedy is that everything goes wrong when we forget this. If the State usurps the first place, the result is tyranny.

If a class stands above God, horrible crimes are then committed in the name of relative morality. If a man puts himself above God, quickly he is destroyed by his pride. Nothing finds its right place until we begin with God.

Unity

For one thing, there can be no unity without God. If there is to be any safety for any of us individually, we must have some sort of social cohesiveness. No man is safe in a civil war and no man can be unconcerned when a revolution is raging in the streets outside his window. The individual has a personal stake in a unified society.

One of the most impressive things about our contemporary life is that we have obtained what we thought we wanted. Ever since the Renaissance, we believed that what we wanted most was power. We have it in unlimited quantities in the atom. Ever since we began to discover the laws of the physical world, we visioned a time when we could make nature serve us. And when that time arrived, many a thinker believed that the main problems would be solved. According to the ideas of orthodox liberalism, we should be living in Utopia right now, where everyone is happy because everyone has enough. That was supposed to eliminate dissension.

How many things we can produce now that our fathers could only hope for! Think about books and our ability to provide them, if you will. There was a time when a Bible was almost priceless, because it took so long to produce by hand. The privilege of reading it for an hour was an expensive one. Today anyone can own a Bible, at least in America. They are often given away and Testaments are available for a few cents. Anyone can write a book, and almost everyone does. They come tumbling off of the presses by the million and yet there is no sign that a new and deeper wisdom has been born. There was a theory that if we could spread knowledge, we would unite men.

Our ability to go long distances in a few moments of time makes us marvel. Just as we get used to what seems an impossible speed, someone develops a machine that doubles it. Contrast our situation with Noah Webster's. In 1785, it took two days for him to travel from Philadelphia to Baltimore, "over a notoriously bad road, in which chasms to the depth of six, eight, or ten feet occurred at numerous intervals. Accidents were so common that the commissioners of the high roads were accused of maintaining a private understanding with the practitioners of surgery." What would Webster have said about a world in which Europe is a few hours away by comfortable, effortless air travel? Surely it would have seemed like a long step in the direction of the good life.

Communication is a miracle. We can go to a football game and listen to another game in another state on a portable radio. To be able to speak easily to people thousands of miles away is surely beyond our understanding. Now we have come to take such things for granted. People talk across the sea or across the continent as easily as we hold conversations with our friends five feet away. The assumption was that this would draw people together and make them understand one another. So much of what we thought we wanted, we have.

Strangely enough, none of these things has brought us together. We are a neighborhood but we are not neighborly. We are bewildered. There is an empty feeling within us. The plain man does not know what has happened. All he can say is what Lewis Browne said in the title of one of his books: "Something Went Wrong."

Now Christianity knows what went wrong. Dr. Elton Trueblood summed it up in a quotation from a physicist in one of America's great state universities. This man said that he had come to three conclusions, as he analyzed our situation. First, there is no salvation in science. Second, we must have a moral renewal. Third, there can be no moral renewal without a living religion to produce it and support it. Isn't it amazing that after we wander all through the new knowledge which has come to the world in the past few centuries, we have to go back to those simple things which the Prophets and Jesus said so long ago? No world of unity without a living faith! No living religion without God! We have to come back to that.

A brilliant New England woman, Margaret Fuller, said one time, "I accept the universe." And Carlyle, who heard of her remark, growled, "Gad she'd better." We had better accept the eternal truth that when God is denied, unity is impossible. We may have all these other things in abundance, but what do they profit us without God? Where the living center of our life ought to be, there is an empty space. It can only be filled by God.

That is true, not only of societies, but of individuals. It is true of your life, of my life, and of any man's life. I am impressed by the emptiness in the lives of so many successful people. There was a time when, as a young preacher, I felt timid in the presence of success. I said to myself, "Have I any word to speak to this man or to this woman? They seem to have everything they need." No longer does that feeling come to me. Here is a man who may have obtained what he thought he wanted twenty years ago. He is successful, stands high in his profession, has an adequate income and he is looked up to socially. Yet he discovers that what he truly wants he does not have. He does not possess peace of mind. There are women who have everything they thought they wanted. They have made successful marriages. They have lovely homes, leisure, nice clothes and no financial worries. Still they are at war with themselves. Success is no substitute for God as a unifying center.

I visited a settlement house in Chicago under the auspices of the Episcopal Church. The old priest in charge had been there through the years. He was the kind of man who speaks to you, looks at you, and you say, "This man is a saint." He told a group of city preachers something of his work and of his methods. He told us of the many men who had come to him for help in the years past. Some of them were drunk, some hopeless, some sick. "But whatever their need," said the old priest, "I take them first into the Chapel and there we kneel in prayer. After I have put the burden of the man's need on God, then we talk together and I can help him." To many a social worker this would sound very naïve and useless. To me it had the sound of deepest reality. There is no real healing for any man until God heals him.

G. K. Chesterton said one time: "The sun does not rise because of the rotation of the earth. The sun rises because God says to it, 'Get up.'" Ah, that is true of human life. It is God who must restore us to sanity. It is God who can make us whole again. It is God who can say to us: "Get up and live."

Dignity

In the second place, without God there is no dignity in human life. We are on a vain search for it unless at the beginning we turn toward Him. We are oppressed in this day with what someone has called "the terrible simplifiers." We want to reduce everything to the skeleton simplicity of a syllogism. If by any chance there are factors which refuse to fit the neat proposition, we reinterpret them or ignore them. These simplifiers are the men who say that all Russians are bad and all Germans are beasts. Then they tacitly assume that all Anglo-Saxons are good and all Americans are sincere and honorable. Criminals are bad men. Dispose of them! All juvenile delinquents are bad children. Punish them! Bad people are to have no place inside the boundaries of human concern and love.

These terrible simplifiers are the men who have not learned that there is a depth of longing in every man's being which he has never expressed. They cannot appreciate the miracle of the soul with its strange mixture of nobleness and frustration, of good and evil. They seem unaware that men are both saints and sinners, and the human heart too vast a territory for any man to claim he has explored it all. Is it possible to dismiss people with some simple formula? Only for fools or materialists. "The mind's eye," wrote Victor Hugo in *Les Miserables,* "can nowhere find anything more dazzling nor more dark than in man; it can fix itself upon nothing which is more awful, more complex, more mysterious, nor more infinite."

Yet this process of simplification is going on about us until the contemporary vision of life is distorted. There are brilliant men who are trying to reduce human life to some natural formula. John Steinbeck is doing it. He has the literary ability to write the great American novel, and no writer comes closer to the simplicity of the New Testament style. If only he had something to say! If only he believed something! In a recent book, he tells the story of a handful of people. Pitilessly, he opens them up to show us what they are. Only one of them is admirable. All the rest are lust-driven, fantasy-driven, ego-driven. Steinbeck seems to be saying to us: "That is what human nature is. Strip off its outside veneer and this is what you have. Here is simple humanity. Here is natural man."

Philip Wylie, in a literary tirade against contemporary confusion, pleads for a return to "instinctual man," whatever that may mean. The thesis seems to be that most of our trouble is due to hypocrisy. In contrast, one recalls the complaint of an eighteenth-century French priest that there were no more hypocrites. Is the answer to man's problem an abdication from all that may make him hypocritical if he fails to achieve it? I think not. This is simply the over-simplification of the terrible simplifiers.

Jesus faced facts in human life that were as bad as those observed by our modern critics. If anyone had a right to be disillusioned about human nature, it was Jesus. But there was something he saw which they do not see. He saw God who had made man in His own image. That vision brought another element into the picture. This creature, which can be made to look so ridiculous, appears to have an innate dignity. This two-legged animal, who often yields to his blood lust and has a streak of cruelty in him which puts the jungle to shame, also has a longing for purity and brotherhood. From that day until this, the men who have been undefeatable fighters for human rights have been men whose faith was rooted in God.

Political systems are shaped by their concepts of human nature. Once this concept has been defined, the system rises inevitably. Nazism says a man is part of a herd and he should be treated as a slightly moronic child who does not know what is good for him. Discipline him, and teach him he is important only as a servant of the State. Communism strips men of their spiritual nature and decries their religious longings. It regards man as essentially a consumer and a producer. We have noted in our time how such a system can begin with a high ideal of equality and turn into the worst tyranny of all without God. Democracy rests upon the Christian Gospel's belief in man as a son of God. Upon what other basis are there "unalienable Rights"? If a man can be used as a means to an end, no other man's rights will be as important as his own.

There is a great story in the Old Testament about Ahab, who wanted a little plot of ground next to the palace. It was owned by Naboth, a peasant. The king offered to buy Naboth's land at whatever price he desired. Or, if this did not suit him, he would give him another piece of land much better than the one he had. But Naboth was a stubborn man and strongly attached to the land where his fathers had lived before him, and he refused to sell or trade. Then Ahab's wife Jezebel came into the picture. To her it was ridiculous that the king could not have what he wanted, especially when only a peasant stood in the way. She came from another land without Israel's tradition. She arranged for Naboth to be falsely accused. He was stoned to death and the land reverted to the crown. But when Ahab went down to possess the land of Naboth, the prophet Elijah met him. Ahab's greeting was a significant one: "Hast thou found me, O mine enemy?" Elijah replied, "I have found thee, because thou hast sold thyself to do that which is evil in the sight of Jehovah" (I Kings 21:20).

This was the source of our democratic tradition. Here was the amazing pronouncement that not even the king had the right to override the dignity of a peasant. Why could Elijah speak his word? Because it was the genius of Israel to have learned in an early time that each man's life is precious in the sight of God.

Civilization

You cannot have a civilization without God. You cannot have a creative and continuing culture unless it rests upon a faith and is nourished by it. It is not a surprising thing that we have failed to remember this. It is understandable that science should have become a sort of god to us. It has the power to work the impossible. We live each day in the midst of miracles which have been wrought by science. Because we grow used to these miracles, we lose our sense of wonder at their nature. Many a man who balks at accepting religion because it is not always explainable, lives in the midst of things he cannot explain. But he uses them.

How many people would be allowed to use the telephone,

for example, if first of all they had to demonstrate how it works and describe its prinicples? I, for one, could not use it if that were the test. How many of us have the foggiest notions about what makes a radio program come through the loud-speaker when we turn the button? Some of us would have to confess that we have only very hazy ideas about the automobile. We may drive it, but if anything goes wrong, we shout loudly for help and think we have done well if we can give the mechanic a hazy idea of what happened before it stopped. No wonder that science seemed a hundred times more potent than religion and a much safer basis for civilization.

We have been unable to convince ourselves that the moral law which cannot be seen is as important as the physical laws which can be manipulated for our physical comfort. More important than character is cleverness if our salvation is in science. Does it matter if the man who makes a useful discovery is good or bad? Of what concern to us is the character of the technician? The center of our emphasis has shifted from what a man is to what a man can do.

Yet strangely enough, in this very hour, when all these miracles are wrought, when all this power is ours, when the end of our cleverness is nowhere in sight, a terrible fatalism has come upon us. We talk about the inevitability of a third world war. We buy carloads of magazine trash purporting to foretell the future and inform us as to our lucky days. Astrologists surround our cities like flocks of vultures and astrology is now big business. Surely this is a travesty on all our pride. We have believed ourselves the most advanced generation that ever lived. We have been proud of our intellectual achievements and the glitter of our materialistic civilization. Yet we have become so frightened that our sophistication and smartness fade away before our fear.

Do you want a parallel to this? Go back to the first century which one of the keenest students of that period

described as "a failure of nerve." It was characterized by
the worship of fate and chance. We are like that. In the
very day of our greatest material triumphs, we seem to have
lost our nerve and become fatalists.

Even our humor has gone sour. So much modern laughter
is sad and bitter with an undertone of frustration. We have
lost our ability to find joy in the simple things of life.
Science which can give us power cannot give us the calm
mind. Science cannot restore the joy of life and help us
laugh again. For joy and laughter are the products of
faith. Men can laugh only when they believe. We cannot
live without faith. Civilization is only a hollow shell that
will be destroyed, unless its people believe in its values and
its future.

Some people are saying the Church has failed. Some insist
that Christians have not fulfilled their obligations. Many
are now having a field day heaping abuse on the religious
institutions of the country. I do not deny our failures, and
it would be futile to insist that we are quite guiltless in this
matter. However that may be, our civilization has set its
heart on goals which Christianity warned us were not
basic, and it seems a poor kind of spirit to attack Christianity for having failed us now. All of this kind of bickering
is as senseless as people on a sinking ship arguing about who
is to blame. It would be wiser to man the pumps.

Civilization is not merely externals. It is apparently
something vastly more than skyscrapers, transportation systems, air conditioning. It stands on spiritual foundations.
Civilization cannot long endure on the basis of the temporal.
We must find God again. There was a man of letters dying,
and his servant heard him murmur, "I want, I want my
heavenly Father." Underneath all this fatalism and this joy-
lessness comes the whisper, "We want God." Which is to
say we want confidence again. We want to believe in our
mission as a people again.

In the late William L. Sullivan's autobiography entitled *Under Orders*, there occurs this most important sentence: "So, at the end of a long journey I have come to this: the first article of my creed is that I am a moral personality under orders." You are, and I am, and our civilization is— all under orders. Can we do just as we like? Certainly not. Are we entirely free to decide our own future? Certainly not. There is God and we move and live and have our being under His orders. Whenever a civilization like ours decides to rebel against Him, the mutiny will not last very long. Under orders—your life! Under orders—my life! Under orders—America and Western civilization!

Reconstruction

It is not only the bombed cities of Europe and Asia that must be rebuilt. If that were the case, the job would be comparatively simple. It is not just a matter of cleaning up the rubbish left from the war. It is rebuilding our vocabulary and our ideas. Once again we have to learn the elementary meanings of justice and freedom and truth. It is finding a road back to the place where we took the wrong turning.

Let us think of this in personal terms. We have some idea of what is meant by repentance. We know it is something vastly more than feeling sorry and apologetic. It is not just changing our surface behavior before our friends. It is rather finding a complete new basis for our life. Paul said it was like being crucified and rising again. The Fourth Gospel speaks of being born again. It is the most radical change we can imagine.

We are frightened by what repentance demands, and we deny it for as long as possible. We will put it off as long as there is the faintest chance we may work ourselves out of our dilemma. But when we can no longer dodge the issue, then in desperation we turn to God. At last we find ourselves able to repent, but only because He helps us. We enter into His suffering. In Zagwill's story *The Cockpit*, the Queen comments scornfully on the New Testament phrase, "the peace of God." She says, "As I lie sleepless, I think of the eternal insomnia of God." Her maid is shocked by this remark, but the Queen goes on, "I only quote the Bible, God neither slumbers nor sleeps. Ah, it is the pain of God, not His peace, that passeth understanding." It is often this vision of the pain of God that performs the miracle of transformation.

What about our world today? Are we getting anywhere? We have some wonderful ideas, but nothing much is happening to give us confidence. We continue the same old game of compromise and expediency. We must repent. We must ask Him to help us. If only we can see His pain and His concern, we can let Him do for us the only thing that will bring salvation.

How long before we learn that this is His world and we are His children? Why do we put our faith in armed might now? Of what value is armament? Have we gone mad that we cannot choose life instead of death? Nothing less than repentance will avail to save us. Christianity must make this clear and call men to adjust their lives and their actions to the word: "In the beginning—God."

In the days before the Civil War, a great antislavery meeting was held in New York. A philanthropist by the name of May made a speech against slavery. It was a clear and direct indictment of the slavery system. When he had finished, a Northern merchant stood up and said, "We are not such fools as not to know that slavery is a great evil, a great wrong. A great portion of the property of the Southerners is invested under its sanction, and the business of the North as well as the South has become adjusted to it. We cannot afford, sir, to let you and your associates succeed in your endeavor to overthrow slavery." He and his kind had their way. But the time came when slavery was overthrown with blood. It put a wound in our nation that has never been healed.

Some would use that same argument today. We have given too many hostages to the *status quo,* they say, and the changes would be too upsetting. We dare not adjust our policy to the moral law of God. Our reconstruction program does not take that into account. Then let this be said: We will either adjust our lives to God, or God will destroy us. To rebuild is the most futile thing imaginable, unless we begin with Him. For He is the beginning, and the ending, and the Almighty. The Christian mind begins with God.

III

HIDDEN WRITING OF GOD

"Who do men say that I am?"
MARK 8:27

For nineteen centuries Christians have been trying to answer that question in the text. So much of the theological controversy has been an attempt to find some working agreement in this matter of defining Jesus. It is inevitable that it should have been so and the end is not yet. As long as men live and think, they will be driven to seek words describing who Jesus was and what his ultimate meanings are. Let us hope that the endless quest may not inspire bitterness, but that every Christian will welcome any light that may come from whatever source.

Theology swings back and forth like a pendulum. No man is big enough to grasp the meaning of Jesus in its entirety. No age and no school can ever hold all the truth about

him. Like his teaching, Jesus is evermore the eternal paradox. The refutation of those who insist that Jesus is merely
this or only that is his refusal to keep within those bounds.
He always breaks loose and smashes our philosophical
limitations. The only adjectives that prove satisfactory are
the ones without limitation. He is Christ, or Savior, or the
Word, or the Son. One of the reasons for the Fourth Gospel's
high place in the affections of Christians is its daring to
place him in an eternal setting.

The leaders of lost causes are held in high honor, but
usually their true place in history can be ascertained. Men
who served their own age with devotion may be the objects
of admiration in future ages. But it is limited admiration.
The instigators of great movements have a place in the heart
of all future adherents to the movement. But when we are
trying to describe one who lived and died, yet affects the
contemporary scene more than any living leader, what shall
we say about him? With whom can he be compared? This
eternal stumbling block to the tyrant—this constant inspirer
of the saints—with what measure can he be encompassed?

George Matheson, the blind hymn writer, had this sense
of the unlimited dimensions of Jesus when he said:

> Son of Man, whenever I doubt of life, I think of Thee. Noth-
> ing is so impossible as that Thou shouldest be dead. I can
> imagine the hills to dissolve in vapor and the stars to melt in
> smoke, and the rivers to empty themselves in sheer exhaustion:
> but I feel no limit in Thee. Thou never growest old to me.
> Last century is old, last year is an obsolete fashion, but Thou
> are not obsolete. Thou are abreast of all the centuries. I have
> never come up with Thee, modern as I am.

Out of the past there has come a memory that has been
helpful to me in thinking of Jesus. There is nothing in it
that will start a new school of thought or disprove an old
one. I set it down in the hope that another may be helped

when he tries to answer the question: "What think ye of Christ?"

I remember going through a period of writing with invisible ink. There was a time when the boys of my neighborhood took to writing notes in some simple chemical solution. Oftentimes, as I remember, it was lemon juice. We were influenced by spy yarns and the desire for a secret society open only to the initiated. Words in invisible ink became much more important and added an element of conspiracy and mystery to our society. Many of you, I suspect, have been through a similar experience and remember it with pleasure.

As we grow older, and perhaps wiser, we discover that much of the truth of living seems to be written in invisible ink. Until we can apply a reagent, it remains unreadable. How else can one explain the opposite interpretations that come from the same set of facts by equally intelligent and sincere people? It is not just a matter of willfullness or stubborn blindness. The truth is that some people see things that others cannot see. Or to put it in harmony with our figure, it is as if some men had the power to touch a blank page with a substance that makes it reveal its hidden writings. And others, unfortunately, have no such power.

There was an astronomer who said that he had searched the heavens very carefully, but he could find no trace of God. Yet the author of the 19th Psalm, without any of the astronomer's instruments, declares with assurance: "The heavens declare the glory of God." The Marxist reads history and assures us that there is nothing there beyond a continual struggle for economic goods. But the Prophets looked at history and saw within it the drama of God's activity and the pattern of His evolving purpose. Paul reminded the Jews that God was in history, and Jesus' coming was a part of His inevitable plan. The Behaviorist regards human nature as a bundle of automatic responses to stimuli. The psychoanalyst reveals our motives as dark hypocrisies, furtively stealing forth from the jungle of the subconscious. But the letter of First John says: "Beloved, now are we children of God, and it is not yet made manifest what we shall be" (3:2).

Certainly this is a strange thing. Why do we not have the same impression when we look at the same object? It is as if one man looked at the page and insisted that it is blank, or at most covered with inconsequential scrawls. His neighbor looks over his shoulder and insists that there are great words written there which speak a vital message. Always when God speaks there are those who will insist that it only thundered. Elizabeth Barrett Browning described it thus:

> Earth's crammed with heaven,
> And every common bush afire with God;
> And only he who sees takes off his shoes;
> The rest sit round it and pluck blackberries.[1]

The great servants of the race are the interpreters. The world has always been at least half-conscious of this, and in the long run, it has honored those able to reveal the hidden truths. The rulers of tomorrow are the revealers. Not always are they heeded at the moment, but the lasting heroes of any age are its seers. Such men have not been confined to any single calling. They have been poets, saints, artists, scientists, philosophers. The thing which they had in common was a disciplined insight which made their lives and their work prophetic.

The artist, by putting one figure, one scene, one incident, one object, on a small piece of canvas, provides a window opening on a universal meaning of life. He uses symbols which not only stand for ideas, but lead the mind into the hitherto unexplored. Van Gogh has a picture of a pair of shoes—just a rough pair of old brogans, worn and scarred.

[1] Browning, "Aurora Leigh," bk. vii.

Yet they tell an eloquent story of simple living and hard toil, until one can see the rough old peasant who wore them. But that is not all. The shoes stand for something universal. They reveal a social situation and a kind of life statistics and surveys cannot make real. They speak of sorrow too deep for words and tell a tale of the sadness of human life.

The poet takes one incident or one observation and in a few lines makes it the symbol of reality. The poem becomes a vision of a principle of the universe in which one can place his trust. Sometimes the reading of a few lines will suddenly clear the mystery away, and in one glorious moment, one sees into the heart of things. Like "The Lost Chord," the vision may never come again, but its memory changes a man's life forever. The poet is always supplying some spiritual alchemy to extract the hidden writings of the universe.

Music brings into experience a new dimension which reveals. In *Midnight on the Desert* J. B. Priestley writes of his last meeting with Arnold Bennett at the close of a concert in Albert Hall which had concluded with Beethoven's *Eroica*. The two men met in the lobby and Bennett said, "Well, Priestley, it lifts you up, it lifts you up." Perhaps that is the best way to say it. Music lifts one up so that he sees things he never saw before. But that is not true for all men. To many of us, music is ever a blank page. We talk with someone who has learned to enter into its most profound experiences, and we know that it says things to him that it does not say, and perhaps never can say, to us.

Books have this quality—at least great books. The deluge of books written by reporters describing the stirring events of the past hectic years, gives us plenty of excitement. But they do not give us revelation, nor does the pattern of the Eternal emerge from them. Generation after generation turns to the classics to rediscover for itself these visions of the meaning of human experience. The test of a great book is its power to illuminate the obscure. Strangely enough, once the writing is made plain, it strikes an immediate note of response in our hearts. It is as if we really knew it all the time but we had to wait for someone to say it for us. The Bible stands as the greatest book of all, for more than all others, it reveals what we are and what potential possibilities we have in us.

In an important literary manifesto published in 1915 and entitled *America's Coming of Age*, Van Wyck Brooks wrote:

> A people is like a ciphered parchment that has to be held up to the fire before its hidden significances come out. Once the divisions that have ripened in a people have been discerned and articulated, its beliefs and convictions are brought into play, the real evils that have been vaguely surmised spring into the light, the real strength of what is intelligent and sound becomes a measurable entity.

To do this, Brooks thought, was the high calling of literature.

Every man has those experiences in his own life which become for him the drawing aside of the veil. It may be a personal relationship, especially a marriage relationship. To love is not merely to put on rose-colored glasses. It is to have the vision of the soul sharpened. To the lover of nature, a view from the mountain or a walk by the sea may clear the dark glass. Worship, when it is profound, takes the worshiper straight to the heart of truth. When prayer reaches its deepest level, which is the willingness to listen and the desire for communion, the light dawns.

Very often, however, the experience which is most revealing is suffering. The worst is usually able to uncover more than the best. These are the experiences one can never describe precisely and they are not easily talked about. A man only knows that before it happened, he did not understand, but now he does. At the funeral service of a loved one, how the great passages of scripture shine with a new light! We may have heard those words read so many times that they are almost memorized. Yet they had to wait until our spirits were baptized with sorrow before they could really speak to us. After having one of these experiences, a man knows that he is forever different, because what he regarded as a blank page is now filled with writing.

All of this is of the utmost importance. For that men should slowly and persistently be led toward understanding "the master-lesson and the riddle's key," is the glory of human life and the sign of man's significance. But art is not enough, for to the man in the street it is always fragmentary and often just beyond him. He feels that he needs something clearer, something more penetrating, something more revealing. Certainly we need something more than isolated data and scientific descriptions. Quiz programs may be amusing, but they are not much help in finding a way of life. The man whose mind is full of facts is not necessarily wise. We do not need to know all of the answers, but we need at least a clue to the answers that really matter. At the very least, we need to be taught how to ask the right questions.

An unprepared schoolboy, willing to risk an ingenious guess, was asked, "What is the Matterhorn?" He answered, "The Matterhorn is a large horn to be blown when something is the matter." The world is full of that kind of sound, but we are in need of a word from men who have seen into the heart of our disease and can announce a healing prescription. We need to go beyond complaints to a cure.

We cannot believe that God will willingly keep His children in darkness and ignorance. Surely He must be anxious to help us see His meaning even as we are to seek it. Sometime, when we are able to bear it and comprehend it, God must send us His supreme interpreter. And that is precisely what Christianity claims to have happened in Jesus. When we dare to apply Jesus to the mysteries of our existence, we see enough to live with assurance. To put it crudely, Jesus is the perfect reagent to bring out the hidden writing of God. It has been said in many different ways, but the faith underlying all expressions is that Jesus carries the revelation to completion where the partial insights leave off. W. Crosby Bell once correctly affirmed that "in all further reflection a point is always reached where, before further progress can be made, something must be done." When God reached that point, he sent Jesus Christ who was His revealing action, making our further progress possible.

History

Jesus reveals the meaning of history. That problem has come before us with a new urgency today. The optimistic belief in history as the story of the inevitable, gradual progress of humanity has been discarded by most serious thinkers in the face of happenings which obviously disprove it. The blindly deterministic movement upward and onward, once preached with fervor by some interpreters of evolution, seems incongruous in the light of the tragic happenings of our time. Many have swung to the other extreme and proclaimed that the story signifies nothing and the search for meaning in history is doomed to failure from the beginning. Cynically, we are told that the more things seem to change, the more they remain the same, without point or purpose.

During the war, Professor Paul Tillich wrote in an article published in *Christianity and Crisis*:

> Seldom in history have men been as disturbed about history as we are today. We urgently want to have at least a glimpse of the future, some wisdom, some prophecy. . . . Furthermore, the great majority of men are longing for an illuminating and profound word about the future of mankind. But those who

have the power to shape the future contradict each other in practically all fundamentals. . . . Those who must speak to the enemy (as I myself have done by radio for the hundredth time this week) realize that on the political plane they cannot say one word of real promise.

But what about the Christian plane? Our religion is committed to the belief that history has meaning and must be taken seriously. It believes that history is a field of God's activity. That belief is rooted in the Old Testament, but most of all it springs from the Crucifixion and Resurrection of our Lord. On his contemporary level, he was only a humble peasant whose life was devoted to the teaching of love. He died in what seemed utter and final defeat. What will history do with him? Forget him? Ignore him? Or will it keep him as a museum piece to illustrate futility and failure?

Well, history seems to be an acid which eats away everything of passing value and leaves only the eternal products. It is discovered that the boasting demagogues and all-powerful tyrants, and the men who make the biggest impression on their own times, are not always the men who possess the future. History is the story of blasted reputations and the complete reversal of contemporary judgments. A returned soldier was showing an old Connecticut Yankee some of the Hitler medals he had brought home as souvenirs. The old man held them in his hand—the Iron Cross, the Swastika. "They're symbols," said the soldier. "I took them from dead Nazis." The old man finally handed them back and said, "I allus wondered what the Good Book meant by soundin' brass an' tinklin' cymbals."

When Luke set down the story of Jesus, he dated it in the days of Caesar Augustus, "when Quirinius was governor of Syria." But who was he? Luke and his contemporaries knew that he was a prominent man and that it would help readers to place Jesus if they knew he lived during this man's governorship. But the years have passed and Quirinius is only remembered because he happened to be about when Jesus was born. That birth became the chronological turning point in history. It was as if men recognized that everything which had happened before his birth was different from anything that might happen after his birth, and should be so noted.

In this respect, Christianity came not to destroy, but to fulfill. Says the Book of Hebrews: "God, having of old time spoken unto the fathers in the prophets by divers portions and in divers manners, hath at the end of these days spoken unto us in his Son" (1:1-2). We must hold this sense of a special redeeming act of God at a particular time in history. This is why the Christian creeds contain such phrases as "born of the Virgin Mary," and "suffered under Pontius Pilate." This is why the Church has branded as heretical all attempts to cut our Faith loose from its historical setting and transform it into a vague mysticism. Christianity affirms that "knowledge of God and knowledge of history are inseparably bound up," writes John W. Macmurray in *The Clue to History*.

When Wendell Phillips visited Plymouth, Massachusetts, he stood on the famous rock. A citizen of Plymouth was boasting of the good fortune of that town in having the rock within its boundaries. Phillips answered him, "I do not acknowledge the right of Plymouth to the whole rock. The rock underlies all America. It only cropped out here." God underlies all of history, but in Jesus that truth cropped out in such a way that we could see it.

Life

Jesus reveals what God has written about human life. Nothing in our experience is so dark and so bright, so complex and so mysterious as our own hearts. It is hard enough to reach conclusions about ourselves, let alone draw conclusions about the whole race. Was the truth about England the quiet, decent family life in the towns and villages, or was it a thousand planes dropping bombs on German cities? Was the truth about Germany Goethe or Hitler? Was it the brutal destruction of Lidice, or von Steuben sharing our struggle for freedom in the Revolutionary War? Is the truth Garibaldi or Mussolini? Tojo or Kagawa? Bilbo or George Washington Carver?

For Christians, the Book of Hebrews gives us an answer: "But we do not as yet see everything subject to him, but we do see Jesus" (2:8-9). After the blood-lust has passed and the hatred has burned itself out, his is the steady pull on our hearts. How did he dare risk basing his appeal on perfection and forgiveness and sacrifice? Certainly it was not blind trust. John has a most illuminating insight:

> When he was in Jerusalem at the festival of the passover, many people believed in his name, as they witnessed the Signs which he performed. Jesus, however, would not trust himself to them; he knew all men, and required no evidence from anyone about human nature; well did he know what was in human nature.   2:23-25, MOFFATT

The One who went to the Cross had no romantic concept of the goodness and trustworthiness of men. He could tell others not to cast their pearls before swine, but he himself was doing it constantly with open eyes. Even at the Last Supper he informed his disciples that one would betray him and that Peter would deny him. Even more devastating than that, he said to them, "All ye shall be offended: for it is written, I will smite the shepherd, and the sheep shall be scattered abroad" (Mark 14:27). Social conditions in the first century were not conducive to excessive optimism regarding the future of society. Whatever Jesus said about men, he did not speak from an ivory tower.

What a horrible time we have been through! What evil we have seen! What cowardice and hypocrisy! When Ribben-

trop referred to the war as "so terrible" at the Nürnberg
Trial, Justice Jackson asked him when the war became terrible to him. Without a smile, but in perfect seriousness,
the Nazi answered, "It became to me terrible—I can tell
you the exact moment. From the moment of the African
landing—I mean of the English-American forces." In
other words, there was nothing terrible about the war until
it began to come home. There are few indications of a
greater moral destruction than testimony like that.

Back of the whole debacle there has been the worship
of false values. The late Dr. Wilhelm von Bode once remarked that Rembrandt in his lifetime painted seven hundred canvases, of which ten thousand are in America. It
is not only in art that we have been satisfied with forgeries.
False promises and broken agreements mark our path, and
no generation has been under such a severe strain as ours
when it comes to maintaining faith in decency. What
monstrous men and programs we have produced!

These past years have been destructive of faith. Yet in
spite of it all, we cannot adjust ourselves to life on this
level. We cannot believe it is normal. We cannot accept
it. All of this goes against a deep-seated, stubborn faith in
ourselves and our fellows. If we could believe that men are
merely barbarous, we could finally adjust ourselves to
barbarity. This we cannot do. We know that war is evil, for
it forces men to go contrary to their real selves and deny
their true natures. Even those who try most to be blasé about
brutality betray themselves by overdoing it; they protest too
much.

In the last analysis, it is true that our ideas of human
nature will depend on what we are and what we have accepted. It is ultimately a matter of faith, and we can believe
about others neither more nor less than we can believe about
ourselves. For Christians, the experience of Jesus is so universal and so overwhelming that they can never escape the

belief that he is the truth about human life. As Adolph Monod, the seventeenth-century French preacher said: "It is only the petty in us that is against Jesus Christ, all that is great in us is on his side."

At a meeting of Alcoholics Anonymous, a man was relating his defeat and final victory over alcohol. He had been one of the seeming hopeless cases. He told how one time he had wanted to buy a very fine watch. It had a stop watch, a chronometer, and it showed the phases of the moon and the day of the month. "In fact," he said, "all it lacked was hot and cold running water." But he knew that a watch like that could not be fixed by the ordinary jeweler. When a repair was needed, the watch would have to be sent back to the maker. "Then one day," said this man, "it came to me that my life was a very complicated affair like that watch. It had broken down. It was out of control. I decided that my only chance was to take it back to its Maker."

When life breaks down, it has been the experience of Christians that Jesus Christ can restore it. When faith is gone, he can bring it back. When we can no longer believe in our own goodness nor in any man's, we can believe in him. Once we dare to look at life through his eyes, our despair turns to hope.

God

Finally, Jesus reveals the truth about God. This is not to say that in Jesus we have the circle drawn and the boundaries set. It is to say that in Jesus there is given the directions and the signs. In him is found the assurance that God meets men. The journey to God is not over when men discover Jesus, but the certainty that the journey is meaningful and the goal obtainable becomes their victorious possession. It is this experience that makes the Fourth Gospel proclaim: "Have I been so long time with you, and dost thou not know me, Philip? he that hath seen me hath

seen the Father: how sayest thou, Show us the Father?"
(14:9). We have learned that what we want to see in God,
we have seen in Jesus.

Christianity would agree that men catch visions of the
meaning of His writing in many different places. Men as
far apart as Wordsworth and Admiral Byrd have spoken of
the sense of an unseen Presence among the English lakes
or on the frozen wastes of the Antarctic. At its best, this
nature experience has brought peace and quietness of spirit.
Sometimes it brings wisdom, as it did to Thoreau. At its
lowest, it has brought a pantheistic conception of a God who
was little more than "an oblong blur." Men have glimpses
of God as projections of their own best selves. They may see
Him in history as a power upholding the moral law for
man and nations.

But all of this does not reach the center of our lives. We
do not need to know about Him so much as we need to
know Him. It is the faith of Christianity that through Christ,
God offers Himself to men. "He shall baptize you in the
Holy Spirit and in fire," says Luke (Luke 3:16). "The Word
became flesh," (John 1:14) is John's way of saying it. In
the centuries which have followed, millions have acted on
this Great Hypothesis, and they have found God. Jesus
stands as the source of that greatest of human experiences—
entering into relationship with God. His promise was that
by acting on his revelation, we would do even greater
things. True it is that the Christian Church has healed more
people through its mission hospitals, helped more poor
through its social activities, and reached more with its
preached word than he did. Yet all of it does not compare
with Jesus' brief life, whose contribution is the constant renewal of our minds and our vision of God, because of what
he was.

In 1781, William Herschel saw the planet Uranus through
a telescope. On the basis of accepted laws of planetary

motion, he plotted its course. But observation showed that
Uranus did not behave as the laws indicated, which meant
that either the laws were wrong or there was an unseen star
causing it to deviate from its course. The latter hypothesis
was accepted by the leading astronomers and Leverrier
worked out the location of the invisible star. Finally, with
a new improved lens, the German astronomer Galle actually
saw Neptune, the planet which had caused Uranus to behave as it did. But long before men actually saw Neptune,
they acted on their faith that it was there.

So, through the years men have known that unless all of
their experience was false, and the history of their race
insane, there was in their universe an unseen Presence who
desired fellowship with men. But there was one who saw
Him so clearly, and described His writings so convincingly,
that men had their eyes opened. Through him, they too,
could see. About the center of that experience, we have
built our faith to live by. We have entered into his mind.
Once we were blind, but now we see.

IV

GOD PRESENT WITH US

> *"But the Comforter, even the Holy Spirit,*
> *whom the Father will send in my name,*
> *he shall teach you all things . . ."*
>
> JOHN 14:26

The announcement of a sermon on the subject of the
Holy Spirit, will not cause a thrill in the hearts of many
modern churchgoers. Once in a while some person gets
curious concerning the words in the creed, "I believe in the

Holy Spirit," and makes a few discreet inquiries. But on the whole, this doctrine is one of the neglected ones.

We may have a vague memory that there was a great controversy between the Trinitarians and the Unitarians. But it is not very clear to us, and anyway, we assume that such things belong to the past. There is a Unitarian church in most American cities, and so far as can be observed, the people who attend there are very much the same as run-of-the-mill Congregationalists or Presbyterians. So far as most laymen are concerned, it would be as difficult stirring up a controversy over the Trinity as over infant damnation.

The Unitarians had a point. They were striving to maintain the Christian emphasis on God's unity. They objected, and I think rightly, to such phrases as "God in Three Persons" found in Reginald Heber's otherwise great hymn. It was easy to fall into the habit of thinking of three Gods instead of one. If those who were champions of the Trinity had kept the emphasis on different aspects of One God, much argument and bitterness might have been saved. Not many would have objected to Brunner's word that "the echo of the word of Christ in our hearts, as the speech of God in us, is the Holy Spirit."

The Holy Spirit is essentially an experience. Judaism spoke of God's Spirit, which meant God's action. The early Christians spoke of Jesus Christ and the Spirit without any clear line of separation. Today, we are aware that "warm, sweet, tender, even yet a present help is He." But like all great experiences, this demands definition and that is when we get the doctrine. We go wrong when we make too rigid what men have said about the experience. Almost inevitably, when we try to tell others what God's Spirit does in human life, we either personify it or semipersonify it. We will do well to remember that we are talking about God and not someone outside of Him.

What we are trying to say primarily is that God acts in

human life. What Jesus was to his contemporaries, the Holy Spirit is to every generation. Somehow, the coming of Jesus made it possible for God's Spirit to act in the human sphere as was never before possible. In Sophocles' tragedy, *Oedipus the King*, there is a soothsayer named Tiresias. He is blind but he sees doom coming on the city. In spite of his warnings, neither the people nor the king will listen. Finally, he washes his hands of the whole business and says, "I go, having said what I came to say." But the Holy Spirit assures us that God never does that. In spite of our stubbornness, he will not leave us. In the words of one of the more modern confessions: "We believe in the Holy Spirit, God present with us for guidance, for comfort and for strength."

A Convicting Presence

In some ways the Spirit is a dreadful companion. We ask for help and he reveals that we do not really want help. We want appreciation. Or we ask for aid to overcome some fault and he makes us see that our real trouble is self-complacency and pride, which we are not ready to surrender. We only want to get rid of one little fault so we can go back to our feeling of superiority. But the Spirit will not be content to give such comfort. Before we know it, he has destroyed all our guarded assurance.

It is the Spirit that convicts us of our sin. A man invited me to dinner one time, and spent most of the evening telling me that he did not go to church and he was morally better than most of those who did. He told me how many times he had been wronged by churchmen and how many times he had been treated honorably by nonchurchmen. At last he came to the point he had been working toward all evening. "I am just as good as anyone," said he. That night as I went home I thought of a man who many centuries ago had caught a vision of God in the Temple. He had cried out: "Woe is me! for I am undone; because I am a man of unclean lips, and I dwell in the midst of a people of unclean lips" (Isaiah 6:5). Ah, the Holy Spirit does not always bring comfort. Sometimes he comes like a fire to burn out our complacency.

Walt Whitman wrote about his preference for animals over men. Cows are calm and placid. They do not whine over their condition. They do not weep for their sins. They do not discuss their duty to God. He could have said it even more simply: they are not troubled by the Spirit of God. They are not superior to men because they feel no guilt, but on the contrary, that placidity is the sign of their inferiority.

Jesus said to the Pharisees, "The publicans and the harlots go into the kingdom of God before you" (Matthew 21:31). At least these despised classes had no exaggerated ideas of their own goodness, and so in Jesus' thought there was hope for them. But for people convinced that they were better than other men, there was no hope, for they were unaware of their need. What Jesus did for first-century Pharisees, the Spirit does for those in the twentieth century.

Let any man come to the end of the day and look back over all the things he said and did not mean. Let him consider the parts he played that were unreal. Let him remember the words spoken he should not have spoken, or worse yet, the words which should have been said and were not. Let him consider his cowardice where there should have been bravery. Then he will know that until he can face all of that honestly, he cannot be made whole. It seems as if the convicting Spirit is anything else except a Comforter. Yet, there can be no comfort for us without first looking at our worst. There is no divine comfort without a claim.

King David was a very great man but he had his weaknesses. One time he fell in love with another man's wife.

He gave orders to his general to have her husband placed in the front line and killed. This was done and David married the woman. But there was a prophet in Israel by the name of Nathan who heard of the affair. He came to David with a story about a rich man with many flocks and a poor man who had one ewe lamb. When the rich man had a special guest, the prophet related, he stole the one lamb from the poor man to provide food for his guest, rather than take one of his own flock. Then said the King, "The man that hath done this is worthy to die." And the prophet replied: "Thou art the man." Just when we think we are safe, the Spirit confronts us with that direct and convicting word.

But we are not only convicted of sin, we are convicted of responsibility. We may raise the cynical question, "Am I my brother's keeper?" Perhaps we have committed no overt act against our brethren. We may assure ourselves that it was this group or that one whose crimes brought on the war and caused our trouble. But there is a sense in which no man is quite innocent. A minister walked down the long corridors of a London military hospital and then turned homeward with this terrible question burning in his mind: "What did you do to prevent this?" He reasoned with himself that he had preached some rather pointed sermons against sin. He had written a few letters. "But did you do all that you could have done?" came the insistent voice. "No," he confessed finally with broken heart, "I too am guilty of this crime."

The difference between political action and religious action lies in this sense of personal responsibility which the religious man feels. The politician says, "There ought to be a law." The Christian says, "It ought to be. Therefore I must become." It is a hard and painful thing to face the evil of the world with my little righteousness. It is much easier to proclaim what ought to be done by the government. But when the Spirit finds me, I know where it all has to begin. Bonaro W. Overstreet puts it this way:

> You say the little efforts that I make
>   will do no good;
> They never will prevail
> To tip the hovering scale
> Where justice hangs in balance . . .
>   I don't think
> I ever thought they would.
> But I am prejudiced beyond debate
> In favor of my right to choose which side
> Shall feel the stubborn ounces of my weight.[1]

This is the spirit of men who, under the impulse of the Spirit of God prefer, if necessary, a high failure over a low success. For what we are and for what we have, we are responsible to God.

The Comforter

Gerald Johnson, historian and writer, plays the flute in the Baltimore Orchestra. In an article in *Harper's Magazine* some time ago, he said that in a certain number of Haydn's, the flute player is supposed to sit quietly for seventy-four measures and then come in exactly on the upbeat of the seventy-fifth. Johnson went on to say that a composer who expects a man to do that is asking for an individual with rare and inestimable qualities.

Life, like the composer, demands people with that ability. Life consists to an amazing extent of the art of coming in at the right time. Our life is not a level process, and our days are not democratic. The author of Second Peter understood it very clearly when in epigrammatical fashion he reversed the word in the Old Testament—"For a thousand

[1] "To One Who Doubts the Worth of Doing Anything If You Can't Do Everything." Used by permission.

years in thy sight are but as yesterday when it is past" (Psalm 90:4) and said, "One day is with the Lord as a thousand years" (3:8). He was saying that there are those moments, those days when, for better or for worse, what we do will affect us for the rest of our lives. That is the way life is. We must simply beat out the time for a long period, but then we are expected to come in at the right moment.

Now for this we need help. Back of a great marriage there is the memory of the husband or wife who, in the hour of crisis, came into the situation and saved it. Many a man would have to say that there were times when he would have gone off the deep end if it had not been for his wife. Marriages have crucial moments when they can be saved only by a husband or a wife who has patience and courage enough for two.

Jesus illustrates this supremely. It was one of his outstanding characteristics to come in when people were meeting an unbearable strain. There was a song older Christians will remember: "Just when I need him, Jesus is near . . . Just when I need him most." He seemed to sense when people were desperate. Remember the story of the Syrophoenician woman with the daughter who was critically ill. She was at the end of her resources, when he spoke his word of assurance and saved her child. There was the story of the woman who had been ill for so long "and had suffered many things of many physicians, and had spent all that she had, and was nothing bettered, but rather grew worse" (Mark 5:26). When every hope had gone, he came in to heal. Or there was the incident of the woman taken in adultery whose life was saved and whose spirit was cleansed in the eleventh hour. There was the dying, repentant thief whose cry was heard by the crucified Christ. There was Peter who to the end of his life was tempted to promise more than he could fulfill, but because his Lord would not let him go, died with courage and honor.

The greatest example of all is the story of the man on the road to Damascus. With blood on his hands and hatred in his heart, he plunged forward on his mad quest for peace. There was nothing on the surface that revealed his need. One would have assumed he had found his mission and was content with the career he had chosen. But there was one who knew better. The eternal miracle happened again and the Spirit came into the situation at the crucial moment and redeemed Paul.

Christianity is not all comfort. It is a disturbing experience and oftentimes a man feels like fleeing from its unbearable tension. The Christian has his mind opened to suffering he never saw before. He knows a sympathy that puts in his heart the pain of the world and on his shoulders the burden of every man. Yet if our religion is only that, we have not arrived at its whole truth. For the Gospel is encouragement and hope. It is a spring of inspiration and joy. It is both a spur and a promise.

Strangely enough, when we try to make our faith all comfort, it refuses to be thus treated. Its comfort comes when we seek first to accept its demands. The most miserable man in the world is the one who has made happiness the supreme goal of his living. Those who have found Life have neither time nor inclination to wonder about how happy they are, anymore than a healthy man desires to keep a thermometer in his mouth to see what his temperature is. The attempt to make Christianity a comforting cult is the sure sign of a sick generation. For an inordinate desire for ease is characteristic of the soft and of the defeated.

The comfort of Christianity always comes as a great, divine surprise. If we do not consciously seek it, suddenly when our need is great the Spirit is there to reassure. Men who have dared the most for Christ's sake are most aware of this presence. Those who protect themselves from the heroic call of their Lord have their reward. But those who have

dared to give God complete sway over them have the gift
of the Holy Spirit, even the Comforter.

"And I will pray the Father, and he shall give you another
Comforter, that he may be with you for ever," saith the
Lord (John 14:16). Down through the years this has been
the experience of Christians. He comes in when we are in
need. He does not always give us the kind of comfort we
think we want. He does not always remove the difficulty.
The thorn in the flesh may have to remain, but the grace
to bear it has been promised. In a sense, this is the heart of
the Good News. What could be better than this? When
things are too difficult, he will give us strength. When we
simply cannot go on, he takes our hand. To every man and
to every woman who will give him his chance, he will enter
the situation with strength and comfort.

That beautiful, courageous, pain-ridden spirit, Frances
Havergal, who had suffered almost all her life, said one
time, "Everybody I meet is sorry for me except myself."
Then she added, "I always see my pain in the light of
Calvary." To those of us who must walk the weary way,
what a great word it is we have to speak. This is the kind
of world where things happen that are not according to
God's will. But there is nothing that happens beyond His
sympathy. The Comforter never leaves us alone.

The Inspirer

A woman came to see me one day to talk about a man
in our community who was very wealthy, very lonely and
very unhappy. She told me he had lived aloof from human
relationships for so long he had become bitter. She had
been a friend of his family for many years and he talked
more easily to her than to anyone else. She wanted to know
if I would see him. But the point of the story is that this
woman had lost her son in an airplane crash just a few
days before. I wanted to say to her, "You are the one in

need. Someone ought to be helping you." Yet it came to
me that here was the Holy Spirit at work. He was healing
her by sending her to another's aid.

This is the way the Spirit works in the hearts of Christians. We are to enter into any situation where there is
needed strength or comfort. Remember Paul's word to the
Corinthians:

> Blessed be the God and Father of our Lord Jesus Christ,
> the Father of mercies and God of all comfort; who com-
> forteth us in all our affliction, that we may be able to com-
> fort them that are in any affliction, through the comfort
> wherewith we ourselves are comforted of God. II CORIN-
> THIANS 1:3-4

It is this truth of the Christian experience which so many
popular modern sects misunderstand. That the Gospel is
to bring comfort to men, is certainly true, but that this is
an experience which is an end in itself, is false. The popular
modern heresies are those which remove the burden from
God's comfort. They let people sit side by side with poverty,
ill health due to poverty, and injustice, without feeling
called on to enter the situation personally. This is the
distortion of the Spirit's ministry of comfort. For we are
to play the part of the Spirit in the lives of our brethren.

Edward Rowland Sill has a poem entitled *Opportunity*.
He writes of seeing a battle on the horizon, in a vision or
a dream. The dust rolled high above the fierce struggle. A
coward sought the battle's edge and wished for a keen
blade such as the king's son carried. But disgusted with his
poor weapon, he broke the old blade and threw it into the
sand. Then he crept away and left the battle. A little later,
there came the king's son, wounded and his lines breaking.
Seeing the broken sword in the sand, he lifted it over his
head with a shout and led his men to a great victory. It
is not to be hoped that all of us will either be kings' sons
or bear their swords. But with what we are and with what

we have, we are commissioned to enter into the battle and
do our part. Many a time it will be our presence and our
word which will save the day.

Never was there a time more significant for Christians to
heed the pleading of the Spirit to enter into the needs of the
hour. We live today with the defeatism of the world eat-
ing away our hope for tomorrow. You can hardly talk to
a man ten minutes without hearing how hopeless he feels
about the world situation. What did we think would happen? Are we so naïve even yet as to believe we could go
through a war like this last one and come out to find everyone hopeful and expectant? We thought that after the experience of the first World War we would be more realistic
this time. But the same whining self-pity begins to take
hold of us again. It builds up until it becomes one of the
threatened causes of our downfall. Let the Spirit help us
to give comfort to the best endeavors being made, and let
us take our place there.

We are in need of patience. The pagan and the materialist
have no patience, for they have no tomorrow. A thing has
to work now or it will not work at all. Either nations must
co-operate now or there is no hope. But the healing of
enmities and suspicions takes time and persistence. Peace
is not built in a day. Our greatest danger is that we shall
be too much influenced by all those who counsel the de-
sertion of the ways of peace and the acceptance of policies
which will make war inevitable. The Spirit can keep us at
our work without losing hope. The Spirit is quiet and constant. For the long and difficult tasks, only men inspired by
the Spirit of God are adequate.

This is the source of our confidence. It is not in diplomacy.
It is in this all-pervading influence working on the hearts
of men everywhere. It knows no racial or national lines.
It never stops its working. It seeks instruments for its activity.

In a recent best-seller, a writer decides to become a Jew in order to find a new angle for a series of articles on anti-Semitism. He announces that he is Jewish and the word soon spreads. He learns how our society is shot through and through with this anti-Semitic poison. As he identifies himself with this minority, he begins to notice things which he had never observed before. At the end of his experiment, he comes to the conclusion that anti-Semitism is not a Jewish problem but a Christian problem, for Christians are in the majority. The minority cannot solve it until the majority are willing to let it be solved. And then this man decides that he will be a different kind of Christian. He will be the kind who acts on whatever front the evil thing shows itself. This, he decides, is the big difference. And so it is!

The most hopeless element in the contemporary scene, in my judgment, is the number of neutral Christians. Churches are filled with people who are perfectly nice but will never lift their hands to battle for a human right. They see evil which embarrasses them, and they look the other way as quickly as possible. They are sorry, but they become clever at not seeing what they do not want to see. Until the time comes when Christians decide that whenever injustice exists that is where they will be; wherever prejudice appears, there they will strike; wherever men are suffering, there they will minister, there can be no solution to our social problems. Christians are not supposed to be bystanders. Norman Cousins was quite right when he insisted that there is no such thing as an innocent bystander. We must be saved from our pious hopes that things will somehow work themselves out and our duty is done when we offer a prayer now and again.

The Holy Spirit inspires us to act. We have thought of it too much as a gentle massage for irritated consciences. It is as terrible as an army with banners in its demand for our response. It takes hold of a man and gives him no peace until he has thrust himself into the human tragedy. When God inspires a man, it is much more than an emotional affair. It is marching orders.

The Protector

When Louis XVIII was deposed from the throne of France, Henry Adams wrote home: "He would have done well in ordinary times but he inherited a revolution, and was not strong enough to stem the tide." We look back on the past and it often appears that countries have been cursed with leadership in times of revolution that might have done well enough if the times had been ordinary. At least the leadership did not know where to turn for aid. We think that if we had lived in times of normalcy, which we always associate with some past period, we would have been able to do what was needed. But the present appears to be too difficult and it strains us beyond our powers of endurance.

The Jews often felt that way and with some reason. There has never been a people who have been expected to bear heavier burdens. To be the chosen people apparently has meant to be chosen for greater suffering. Sometimes they rebelled and declared it was too much. But whenever that mood threatened, their leaders insisted that they were not called upon to do the impossible. Deuteronomy spoke to such a mood:

> For this commandment which I command thee this day, it is not too hard for thee, neither is it far off. It is not in heaven, that thou shouldest say, Who shall go up for us to heaven, and bring it unto us, and make us to hear it, that we may do it? Neither is it beyond the sea, that thou shouldest say, Who shall go over the sea for us, and bring it unto us, and make us to hear it, that we may do it? But the word is very nigh unto thee, in thy mouth, and in thy heart, that thou mayest do it. DEUTERONOMY 30:11-14

It is an assumption in Israel's religion that if God demands something, He will also provide the power for its doing. The Spirit of God does temper the wind to the shorn lamb, as Lawrence Sterne said.

Christians find that a seeming impossibility holds an unescapable fascination for them, as if the Spirit were tempting them to undertake it. About four hundred years ago, a monk came to the conclusion that the Church needed reforming. At that time, the Church was the most powerful institution in the world, and such institutions do not reform easily. With a lonely courage he drew up his indictments and nailed them to the door of the Castle Church in Wittenberg, Germany. Not many would have believed that much could come from that brave act except martyrdom. But as people read those ninety-five theses, they found the same things had been troubling them. Thousands rose to stand beside the monk, not always from the highest motives, it is true. But the Reformation was born when Martin Luther dared to believe that the Spirit's prompting was a guarantee that his dangerous act would not be in vain.

To believe in the Holy Spirit means to believe in the protection of God. We are not tempted beyond our powers to resist. In spite of the modern teaching that men are merely victims of their environment or heredity, Christianity insists that God has drawn a line around us which no destruction can cross. If it ought to be done, that is the sign God knows we can do it. God knows us better than we know ourselves.

We are too fearful. We are afraid to ask very much of men in the name of Christ. Dictators are not afraid to ask ten times as much from people as the Church dares to ask. A friend one time said, "We have taken such good care of our weaker brethren, that they are about all we have left." We need to re-emphasize the doctrine of the Holy Spirit, especially in terms of God's protection over men called to do the difficult thing.

We do not need miracles performed for us. We need to have once again the sense of what can be done by men who are willing to trust the Spirit. A French philosopher said that a breeze will blow out a candle but will only fan a flame. The little, fearful man, who has only his timid candle burning, will find it being blown out by every wind of adversity. But when a man rests in the assurance of the Spirit, the wind, instead of blowing out a candle, fans the flame of his faith into a mighty blaze. For he rests in the assurance that God's power is his to call upon.

Wendell Phillips was a great crusader against slavery in a day when it was not popular to take such a stand. He knew what it was to have the opposition of crowds rise against him with bitterness. He said that one of his greatest helpers in those difficult days was his wife. She was an invalid and could never accompany him on his lecture tours. But always, when he kissed her good-by, she would say: "Now, Wendell, don't you shilly-shally." The memory of that word kept him to his course without compromise. So the Spirit sends us forth to do the difficult thing with a demand, but also with a promise of God's protection.

To be a Christian is to believe in God's Holy Spirit. He convicts us of our sin and responsibility. He comforts us in our hours of stress. He inspires us to act in the human situation in God's name. He protects us against the power of our enemies and surrounds us like a mighty fortress.

V

THE MIND AND THE FLESH

> *"So then I of myself with the mind,
> indeed, serve the law of God; but with
> the flesh the law of sin."*
>
> ROMANS 7:25

We cannot begin any constructive program until we decide for ourselves what man is. A false assumption regarding human nature, means the inevitable failure of all our efforts. What man is both sets the limitation of our planning and constitutes its true testing. We are in no position to patch up the old world or start the building of a new one until we have done the hard and painful job of examining ourselves and deciding what sort of creatures we are.

We have done much talking about our rights as human beings. Since the days of the writing of the American Constitution, we have blithely assumed we had rights which no one could lawfully usurp. In our best moments we have discussed, though not with the same enthusiasm, the duties of man. There is, however, an even more ultimate question. Carlyle's remark concerning the French Constitution of 1789 said it in these words:

> With endless debating, we get the *Rights of Man* written down and promulgated: true paper basis of all paper constitutions. Neglecting, cry the opponents, to declare the *Duties of Man!* Forgetting, answer we, to ascertain the *Mights of Man*; one of the fatalist omissions.[1]

[1] Carlyle, *French Revolution*, I, bk. vi, ch. 2.

This fatal omission has been brought to our attention in recent times by the failure of a shallow liberalism whose faith in the efficacy of secular progress has been relegated to the same shelf with the Glad Girl Stories. We may, just now, be in danger of going to the other extreme and subscribing to a pious fatalism which places all responsibility in the hands of a transcendent Deity. This would leave man quite helpless to have any part in the salvation of himself or his world. We shall get off the horns of this dilemma only by going back to the Christian doctrine of man. The Bible portrays man as a creature of two worlds, which means tension, inner conflict and an endless quest without permanent resting place here. We had better look at that again, and particularly we need to restudy St. Paul.

Some who do not share my enthusiasm for Paul, may ask why we turn back to him. Why not turn back to Jesus? There are several reasons. In spite of the fact that the Apostle puts his thought into abrupt and extreme forms and uses a vocabulary that seems strange to us as well as exaggerated, these very defects (if such they be) help us to see the depths of the issues he is discussing. Other statements are too smooth. We sometimes study the extremes in order to understand the tendencies which are hidden by the normal. No man understood better than Paul the real implications of the religious movement which began with Jesus. He is probably the supreme example of a man defeated and filled with despair because of the insoluble contradictions within his own nature, who found harmony through a religious experience within the Christian faith.

Paul's own interpretation of that experience has had what might be termed a "normative" influence on the subsequent history of our religion. The Christian doctrine of man has been, broadly speaking, based on the seventh chapter of Romans. There has been effective power in his psychology as well as in his theology, and the Church is always turning back to it. The greatness of Augustine and Luther lies chiefly in the fact that they rediscovered Paul during critical periods in the Church's history. Nearly every great revival of Christianity has been, among other things of course, a rediscovery of the Apostle to the Gentiles. It is hardly too much to say that when Christianity has been most effective, it has been the Christianity of St. Paul.

It will seem like an extreme statement to many, but there is a sense in which Paul knew more about human nature than our modern psychologists. At least he knew the right questions to ask and he defined the real issues. Much of our modern study asks the wrong questions to begin with, and so no matter how clever it may be, we never arrive at the answers that are important. A man who could analyze his own heart's need, and who had found where those needs could be satisfied, is wiser than men who know only how to experiment with rats.

The Apostle puts his thought into two main categories. First of all, he speaks of "the natural man," and secondly, he speaks of "the spiritual man." Out of this contrast there has grown the impression that Paul is bespeaking the dualism associated with Greek philosophy. It must be admitted that many Christians have interpreted Paul so that the spirit has been good and the flesh has been evil. Many a modern who thinks this is unhealthy, has developed a prejudice against the Apostle. But a careful study of human nature according to St. Paul, will show that this is not his point of view.

The Natural Man

The natural man is not necessarily a depraved man at all. To read the Letters of Paul carefully is to see that any doctrine of total depravity did not begin with him. He believes too much in men and he is too willing to insist on moral standards for all mankind. The natural man may believe in Judaism and hold to its pure monotheism and high ethical standards. Or he may be a sincere believer in the gods of the pagans, recognizing their demands which he is under obligation to obey.

Such people are all about us in our modern world. They are the decent people outside the Church, and there are many of them. They live up to a fairly high code of morals; they are good neighbors and good friends; they show they have been influenced, perhaps unconsciously, by the Christian culture of our civilization. Yet Paul looked out upon such people and he was very pessimistic because they seemed to him cut off from the source of spiritual power. They were living on borrowed insights, and were in a sense not so far from the Kingdom, but in another sense they were very far from it.

The natural man is one whose duties are painful and unpleasant. The joy of religion he does not know, and while he regards the moral code as something one ought to live up to, there is no real satisfaction in it. He is like a small boy wondering why it is so hard to be good and so much fun to be bad. To him, the religious or moral spirit seems to be gray. As the old lady who could not overcome her habit of getting drunk periodically said to Muriel Lester, "There isn't a better woman in the world than I am. But I just can't live up to it."

It is this natural man who is so tragically dualistic, for he is ever aware of two men within him and two terrible pulls on his will. Psychologists have analyzed these warring personalities within the same man. Novelists have written about them. Paul described them in Romans in a passage which I believe is largely autobiographical:

> For the good which I would I do not: but the evil which I would not, that I practice. But if what I would not, that I do, it is no more I that do it, but sin which dwelleth in me. I find then the law, that, to me who would do good,

evil is present. . . . Wretched man that I am! who shall
deliver me out of the body of this death? ROMANS 7:19,
21, 24

Luther spoke of the same dark problem when he said a
man's heart is like some foul stable. What man has not
been shocked when he looked at the sin and evil in his
own heart?

In general, the natural man is like the alcoholic—full
of good resolutions but without power to carry them
through. Life is too much for him and though he seeks
to put on a good front and keep a calm appearance, down
below the surface there is fear and uncertainty. He is never
sure about tomorrow, and he is a victim of the innumer-
able dangers of weakness. He has no sure defense. Life
overwhelms him, and his social environment controls him.
Cosmic forces, too powerful to curb, have him at their
mercy. And all of this is much worse because it must be
hidden and kept secret.

Aesop has a fable about a cat which was turned into a
woman. She sat demurely at the table until a mouse ran
across the floor. The natural man is always under the
strain of playing a part which is contrary to his hidden
nature. He must pretend to be debonair, with hardly ever
an opportunity to let down his guard and confess his hidden lie. Because he understood all of this, Paul had no
confidence in humanity apart from Jesus Christ. The natural man is a slave, a victim, and in the very hour he
shouts loudest about being master of his fate, he may be
contemplating suicide.

The natural man is the producer of a paradox which
soon or late destroys him. When a society is under his
sway, it hastens to its destruction. Arnold Toynbee quotes
this description of man: "A god in technology; an ape in
life." He goes on to say that this could be man's epitaph.
If it is not to be the last word about humanity, then God

must do for us what he did for St. Paul. God must transform the natural man into the spiritual man.

The Spiritual Man

To Paul, the change that took place in him when Jesus
found him on the Damascus Road was like coming from
death into life. To him it seemed no natural growth but
a catastrophic redemption. It was like being crucified and
rising from the dead. It was, in a word, the kind of experience one might expect would come to a tempestuous genius.
We should be grateful that in describing the experience,
Paul used such sharp, clear terms that we cannot miss his
meaning. Even if the experience does not come to us with
such shattering might, Paul helps us to understand the
meaning of what Christ does for men.

For one thing, the spiritual man knows at last what he
wants and what he needs. A king was discussing a proposed
policy with his counselors. He wanted to be sure that what
he proposed to do was legal. But one of his advisers said,
"Sire, you are not to consider what is lawful, but what
becomes you." It was a well-merited rebuke. If a man is a
king, he acts in accordance with what becomes kingship.
He learns what is proper to his station. Thus does God
deal with men. He does not surround them with legalities
and rules. He brings them a vision of what is becoming.
He gives them the mind of Christ.

It is not too much to say that the spiritual man is saved
by a sense of shame. This is one of the strangest and most
wonderful things about us—we can be ashamed. Why is it
a man can be disgraced in his own eyes when nobody else
knows about his guilty act or thought? None of his neighbors even suspicion it, yet there is such remorse in his
heart that he hungers for pardon. Animals do not have
this sense and its possession makes a man different from
any other creature.

Now the natural man may know shame too. But in his case it is something to hide. He tries to so deaden the remorseful feeling that it will trouble him no more. This thing which could lead him to life and save him is silenced by an indecent fear. The natural man is too proud to be ashamed. His blustering assurance is a pseudo protection for a spirit that is not secure. There is hardly a better example of how the same experience brings life to those who have been found by God, and death to those who are apart from Him.

St. Paul himself must have been made ready by shame for his Lord. The road from Jerusalem to Damascus is not more than one hundred miles, but when Paul traveled it, that was a long distance. It was a monotonous road. There was not much to look at and not much to engage his mind in what he saw. He was forced into communion with his thoughts and his memories. He had just come from the stoning of Stephen. He had watched a man killed by one of the most horrible methods men can use to dispose of their fellows. He had watched Stephen stoned into an unrecognizable pulp. He watched it and felt a morbid satisfaction that another member of this dangerous sect was silenced. But he could not get out of his mind how Stephen had prayed: "Lord, lay not this sin to their charge" (Acts 7:60). And he was ashamed. It was that state of mind that helped him see the light and hear the Voice.

It is certainly a far cry from the story of David in the Book of Second Samuel to modern novels. Most of our contemporary storytellers do not begin with the same assumptions that underlie the Biblical Book. But in spite of that, our modern novels cannot escape making much of the shame that comes to people who betray their own best impulses. I am impressed with the underlying sadness of much present-day fiction, due to the failure of even tough characters to silence their inner voice of shame. This voice does not always lead to repentance and salvation. But when any sensitive writer observes life honestly, he cannot fail to note this common human experience. Whether a man lived twenty-nine centuries ago or yesterday, shame can destroy him or save him. It will depend on the kind of mind he has formed.

Every minister and every counselor has people coming to confess sins committed long ago. They come not because they are in danger of being found out. They come because they have grown tired of hiding secret guilt, and unless they can find some relief from their shame, they are in danger of mental and spiritual disaster. Their coming to confession is perhaps the most hopeful thing that has happened to them in years. If they can be led to reach out for the forgiveness of God, they can be saved. How patient is His Spirit! He will wait through the years for a person to find his shame intolerable and come to Him seeking life.

We can take care of the outside opposition. We are not afraid of our competitors. We are at home in the ruthless struggle of modern business life. But there is something against which we have no defense. That is a feeling for what becomes us and a secret sense of shame at our betrayal of our best selves. When a man decides he cannot bear it longer alone, he is ready for the creation of a new life.

Storm Jameson, the novelist, says that one time in the city of Vienna there was a rabies scare. The city officials decided to get rid of all the dogs running loose without licenses. They hired men with clubs to find such dogs and kill them. One of these men was walking beside the river when he saw a dog without a license. He drew back his club and hurled it, but his aim was too high and the club went into the river. The dog sprang into the river after it and brought it back in his mouth. After running up and down and shaking himself a few times, he laid the club at the man's feet. The man went to the city hall at once and resigned. Against a sense of doing something shameful, he knew there was no defense. For the natural man shame is an embarrassment which is the source of hypocrisy. But when God breaks in, this sense of disgrace can lead a man to life and peace. This does not mean that the spiritual man will never know guilt again. But it means a deeper level has been reached. He dares to acknowledge his humiliation, for he knows a source of forgiveness.

The second thing that happens to the spiritual man is the gift of a new heart. The natural man never lets anything penetrate too deeply. All of his safety lies in maintaining a passable external appearance. Jesus leaned over backward in telling men that the heart was the center of life. It is there that goodness and evil are found, and there the decisions are made. Of what value is the cleansing of the outside of the cup, he asks, when it is the inside of the cup that is unclean. Lust is a thing of the heart and not always a matter of outward act. Murder is done within.

A man may be good outwardly but bad inwardly, and it is his inward badness that is the truth about him. That is why Jesus was so ruthless in his criticism of the Pharisee, and it was why many thought he must be a dangerous lunatic. For the Pharisee was the best man outwardly that Judaism could produce. But Jesus was aware that whenever people put their emphasis on an external following of the law, and the outward ceremonials of religion, they are in danger of substituting those things for inward goodness. A man might walk circumspectly among his neighbors, but because his motive was a dishonest one, he might still be a bad man.

St. Paul learned this lesson well from his Master. He writes in the great thirteenth chapter of First Corinthians: "If I speak with the tongues of men and of angels, but have not love, I am become sounding brass, or a clanging cymbal . . . if I give my body to be burned, but have not love, it profiteth me nothing" (13:1, 3). I think this, too, is auto-biographical. Paul is remembering the sacrifices he made in the name of purifying his religion. He is remembering those hectic days before his conversion, and he knows now that what a man really is, must always be a matter of the heart.

The other side of this truth is that a man may seem to be bad outwardly but he may be good inwardly. There was an old doctor in a town where I lived who was crusty and rude when you spoke to him. Sometimes he would answer and sometimes he would not. Usually, the best one might hope for was a grunt. He did not have a pleasant manner in the sick room. When someone called him in the middle of the night for a stomach-ache, he told the patient what he thought about it. Yet I learned of a deep affection which many of the older people especially had for him. I began to see marks of his kindness in many places. There came to my attention from time to time incidents of free service and generosity. When I really became acquainted with him, I discovered one of the most tender hearts and one of the most loving spirits in any man I ever met.

Jesus summed it all up when he told the parable of the last judgment. The noteworthy thing is that everyone was surprised. The good were not as good as they thought and the bad were not nearly as bad as they thought. Jesus was saying, the decision will be made according to a man's heart, which means that we cannot judge and we must leave the decision to God.

It is the gift of the new heart that is the miracle of God's grace. Not even Jesus tried to explain it. He could only say it was like the blowing of the wind which can be felt but cannot be seen. When He has cleansed our hearts, we like different things; we think different thoughts; we measure with different standards. Studdert-Kennedy, the famous chaplain of the first World War, was preaching to a large congregation of soldiers on Good Friday. At the end of his sermon, which had moved them powerfully, they broke into thunderous cheers. The chaplain himself was taken aback. "It sounded strange," he wrote home, "to hear men cheer Christ, strange to us and not perhaps what we would do, but you would have loved it, and so, I am sure, did He." It is the new heart that makes us cheer for Christ, and what we cheer for deep within us, is the measure of our lives. Nothing can be done to deserve the gift. We cannot command our affections at will. That is why the spiritual man walks always in a kind of blessed wonder. He only knows it happened at God's command and by His power.

Christianity in its most profound manifestations is power. The despair of the natural man lies in his knowledge, barely admitted to himself, that he is not quite up to life. He can handle it if all goes well. But when he looks around at what has happened to some of his brethren, he is afraid that he could not possibly endure it. Now the spiritual man has no advantage over his natural brother, so far as controlling the future is concerned. But the spiritual man has faith that he can call on spiritual power to conquer or to endure. Dean Sperry of Harvard writes:

> Liberal Protestantism is out of touch with the whole Pauline conception of the Christian life, not because it cannot translate Paul's rabbinical ways of thought but for a far deeper reason. It is not accustomed to think of the initial commitments of the Christian life as above all else the quest for power, the power which saves us from ourselves and from the world, and makes us, out of weakness, strong.[2]

And that is one of the main reasons why liberal Protestantism needs to get back to Paul.

Christianity does not put its faith in commands and rules. What law can do is very limited when it comes to affecting human life. We have to be reborn. If you will

[2] Sperry, *Reality in Worship*, Macmillan, 1925.

look at the New Testament, you will discover that Jesus did not talk very much about what men ought to do. The word "ought" in the sense of obligation only occurs three or four times in the Gospels. Dr. Harry Emerson Fosdick pointed out some time ago that the Greek word meaning "ideal" does not occur at all in the New Testament. It is not a Christian word. If Jesus did not go about telling people what they ought to do and defining ideals for their behavior, what did he talk about? The answer is that he talked about what men are. He kept saying to men as the counselor said to the king, "You must do what becomes you." He did not try to lift men by whipping up their sense of duty. He tried to make men aware of what they were.

It is a strange truth that men need help in understanding themselves. The world is so full of siren voices and alluring byways that a man can lose his way completely. We can become our own worst enemies. We can spend our lives following after what we do not really want. Sometimes when we stand on a high cliff, we feel a power drawing us to the edge. Life is full of attractions which lure us over the abyss. Christ comes to clear our visions and define us for ourselves. He surrounds us with God's protection and love. Paul said it best: "For I am persuaded, that neither death, nor life, nor angels, nor principalities, nor things present, nor things to come, nor powers, nor height, nor depth, nor any other creature, shall be able to separate us from the love of God, which is in Christ Jesus our Lord" (Romans 8:38-39).

The truth which the New Testament relates so clearly is that men in Christ find God, and feel flowing through them the immense and immeasurable strength of the Almighty. They have found God, or better, they have been found by God. With this central experience, all of life falls into a meaningful order. We begin at the real beginning and

work toward the real goal. The spiritual man is neither
perfect nor static. He has achieved neither finality nor
passive relaxation. He is still faced with dilemmas. But he
knows at last that there is enough power available if he is
willing to pay the price of surrender to the will of God. In
that faith is his salvation, for God has become not a last
resort but a constant Presence. He must begin with self-
despair, for the spiritual man cannot be born until the
natural man faces his own incompetence and hopelessness.
The new man is born when we have overcome our "ignorance of our own ignorance" and had our self-sufficiency
shattered.

At the close of a great meeting held by Dwight L. Moody,
a young man came up to him and said, "Mr. Moody, you
moved me greatly tonight. I feel I would like to be a
Christian. But I'm afraid that I cannot give up my undesirable companions. What shall I do?" Moody waited a
moment and then he said, "Young man, you just decide to
live a Christian life, and your undesirable companions will
give you up."

It is as simple as that. The natural man looks at all the
pitfalls ahead and all the temptations which await him. He
shrinks from commitment to the Christian way. But when
the miracle has been performed and the natural man has
become a spiritual man, most of these dangers pass him
by. The spiritual man knows the seriousness of sin. But
he has been given a new mind. Now he knows also the
adequacy of Jesus Christ.

VI

TO SEEK AND TO SAVE

*"For the Son of man came to seek and
to save that which was lost."*

LUKE 19:10

*"And if thy right eye causeth thee to
stumble, pluck it out."*

MATTHEW 5:29

The words of Jesus do not find us until we are prepared for them. The contemporary mood is always a sort of censor so far as he is concerned. Automatically we turn from the part which does not seem to say what we want to hear, and emphasize the teaching which seems best to fit the present need. There is no sense in talking to people about a power sent from God to seek and save the lost, if they do not think they are lost. Salvation is a vital subject only to the needy.

Today, we know we are lost—at least most thinking people know it. We may not agree with the causes of our failure or what lies in store for us in the future, but most of us can agree that all is not well. The more sensitive we are to our situation, the more alarming it seems to be. If the offer of salvation is announced now, it can be sure of a respectful hearing.

Sin now seems to be more than a wrong choice or a temporary hindrance. It is more than infringement on the taboos of a deity. It is more than ignorance. Once again it seems like something black and tragic. It is all the evil which shuts us off from God and life. It is a force which seems to be driving us to suicide. It is an immense, invisible power which we do not know how to grapple with because we cannot reach it or understand its nature.

It manifests itself in personal life as a loss of individual significance and dignity. Sin and death bring to us a terrible loneliness as we contemplate the passing years and our little time remaining. It is not only something that attacks the ignorant, for educated men are not safe from this sense of lostness. E. B. White expressed this in a comment he made at the time of Knute Rockne's death. President Hoover sent a eulogistic message and White wrote:

> We see nothing wrong in the President's expressing grief over the loss of a beloved football coach, but from a diplomatic angle, it seems to leave out certain other deceased members of college faculties, men who worked with undergraduates in groups other than groups of eleven. In our unofficial capacity, therefore, we take this opportunity to express the nation's grief in the death of all the other upright members of college faculties who died during the past year. We are sorry we don't know their names.

The world is full of nameless, lonely, defeated people.

Ah these nameless ones! In sheer desperation they have cheered the obscene dictators and worshiped the State in order to escape their anonymity. They allow their critical faculties to atrophy and are the fair prey of every demagogue. Because they are emotionally starved, they can be emotionally controlled. They have tried all kinds of tricks and have listened with hope to all kinds of promises. But in the quiet moment of their solitude, they know it is all in vain. They have not found meaning for their existence, and they are hopeless and frightened.

The alcoholic is in some ways the symbol of our lost generation. It is a rather startling thing that several of our best sellers in the last few years have had alcoholics as their heroes. Certainly this must mean something about us. Does it mean that in the alcoholic's pathetic failure to find an answer to the impossible tensions of life, we see ourselves? Does it mean that we can no longer number our days with soberness? However much or little we may make of this phenomenon, it is surely a sign of our need for salvation.

The Divine Initiative

The older preachers of a past generation made salvation the center of their message. This is to me the most striking thing about their sermons. With what is almost a monotonous regularity, they always came around to offer salvation to every man in the congregation, in the name of Jesus Christ their Lord. John Henry Jowett is a good example. Within the last year I have read everything he wrote. The great impression that remains with me is his assurance that he had good news indeed. There was no hesitation on his part in assuming that men needed to hear his good news. Perhaps all of us, ministers and laymen alike, need to follow his example. For if Jesus Christ can seek and save the lost, that needs to be proclaimed with power.

Those who have been saved by Christ from the futility of life are always impressed with the wonder of it. They always want to say, "How could it happen to me?" It seems almost beyond belief that God is willing to redeem any man's poor life. In "Ballad of Judas Iscariot" Robert William Buchanan talks about this experience. The scene is the serving of the Holy Supper in a lighted, warm room. But the Bridegroom hears weary footsteps outside and the moan of a tired soul. Finally, when he insists that he must know who it is, one of the guests mutters fiercely that it is the soul of Judas Iscariot. Then the Bridegroom opens the door and beckons. When at last the trembling, fearful Judas steals in, he hears these words:

> The Holy Supper is spread within,
> And the many candles shine,

And I have waited long for thee
Before I poured the wine.[1]

If in our imagination we can enter into the emotions of
Judas at that moment, we shall know something of the
feelings of men who have been sought and found by Christ.

Who can define what the saved man has experienced?
We are driven to say in a kind of despair, "None but his
loved ones know." It is the experience of wholeness and
unity. Our broken wills are made strong again. It is the
feeling of at-homeness. No longer do we feel like lost souls
in the dark. Life means something again and we mean something. We are ennobled. We look forward to every new
day's experience with expectancy. St. Paul is speaking for
every man who has found Christian salvation when he says:
"Wherever I go, thank God, he makes my life a constant
pageant of triumph in Christ" (II Corinthians 2:14, Mof-
fatt).

The songs of praise which rise from the hearts of the
redeemed always seem exaggerated to the unredeemed. So
much of the testimony of the saints is simply so many words
to the pagans. For underneath them there is this indescribable experience. The sign of salvation is the assurance and
joy which possesses men even in the midst of evil times. They
want to say with Charles Wesley:

O for a thousand tongues to sing,
My great Redeemer's praise.

The Human Side

Now when we seek to analyze this revolutionary experience of salvation, it seems to consist of two main parts.
There is no doubt but that it comes from God and we know
that "while we were yet sinners, Christ died for us" (Romans
5:8). But there is demanded also a human response which
has often been minimized and neglected. There is no value

[1] Quoted by John Erskine, *The Human Life of Jesus*, Morrow, 1945.

in suggesting that men can be saved easily and effortlessly. Salvation is painful, and its difficulty was never covered over by Jesus.

There is a passage in the Sermon on the Mount where he describes this side of being saved. He says:

> And if thy right eye causeth thee to stumble, pluck it out, and cast it from thee: for it is profitable for thee that one of thy members should perish, and not thy whole body be cast into hell. And if thy right hand causeth thee to stumble, cut it off, and cast it from thee: for it is profitable for thee that one of thy members should perish, and not thy whole body go into hell.　　　　　MATTHEW 5:29-30

This is indeed a hard saying. But the Gospel is not a sentimental view of life. We have become allergic to this kind of teaching and have simply neglected it. But it is a part of the Christian teaching about salvation.

We are proficient at hanging on to things we want to keep and ignoring unpleasant truths. Macaulay told a story about a Hindu who had always believed it was wrong to eat any kind of living creature. He preached the gospel of vegetarianism with vigor. One time he was shown his vegetable diet through a microscope. Did this change his view? No, he smashed the microscope. Today we had better look honestly at what salvation asks of us. There are demands which will be as difficult as plucking out an eye or cutting off a hand. But when a world has drifted as far toward the edge as ours has, only extreme methods will be enough to save us.

Society

For one thing—how shall the nations be saved? National survival now demands that we cut off practices as precious to us as our hands. The most distressing thing about the political situation is the number of men in places of power who do not have the foggiest notions of the real issues at stake. They cannot see what we must do to be saved. They spend their time discussing silly little inconsequential things while the world burns. With their eyes on the next election, they pander to pressure groups and indulge their personal animosities. There are certain notable exceptions, it is true, but in a day when we need physicians who can diagnose our sickness, we have too many quacks with only pleasant bedside manners.

If we want to be saved, we must pluck out our nationalistic ideas of sovereignty. Certainly the United Nations has undesirable features within its structure. Single great powers can halt constructive programs and there are other obvious weaknesses. But one of the main reasons it is weak is because the great powers, America included, show a tendency to keep an unredeemed sense of their sovereign right to do as they please. If we by-pass the United Nations, we have contributed to its failure.

No one should be so naïve as to think it will ever be easy to deal with a system like Russian communism. It is never easy to deal with any self-consciously great power. If one thing seems certain, it is that unilateral relationships are no longer practical. The only possible hope we have lies in establishing a pattern of world action upheld by world public opinion. It is nice to be powerful and settle things in our own way and by our own methods. But unless we throw our weight behind the slower, more painful processes of the United Nations, we cannot be saved.

God is saying to us that if we cannot destroy our isolationism, we cannot go on living. You say that there are no isolationists left? They are not in the open yet and they call it something else. But most of us shudder when we think of the high cost of co-operation and the bill which we will have to accept as the price of our power. What man among us does not wish it were possible to look after only our own country? Who does not long for lower taxes? It is a safe prophecy that soon or late there will be a great wave of protest against further investment in other countries. But if we heed this protest, we are lost. Salvation now demands that we bear responsibility for all mankind, or with all mankind, go into the outer darkness.

To those who have ears to hear, there is a Voice saying that unless we can destroy our selfish individualism there can be no salvation for us. Is anyone proud of what has happened to us economically since the war? We were in a hurry to get back to what has been termed "free enterprise." We had endured government control and regimentation long enough. Quite so! But the orgy of selfishness which has characterized all groups and all classes, makes us wonder if anything like free enterprise is possible for such undisciplined people. What a shameful sight it is to see people clamoring to get theirs while they can, even when that path leads to ruin.

None of us wants a totalitarian regime. We want as much individual liberty as it is possible for us to have. We want to walk the straight path between the anarchy of unrestricted individualism on the one hand, and state domination on the other. But the amount of our liberty must necessarily rest on the amount of character we can produce. If we cannot rule ourselves, we will be ruled from above, and in that direction lies tyranny. If a democratic way of life is necessary for the fulfillment of human destiny, then we can be saved only if we root out our selfishness.

We must pluck out our divisions and our selfish pressure groups. There is something more important than any group in America, and that is America. There is something more important than America, and that is the world. We must say to every tribe and clan that we can no longer consider less than the whole. We are all members, one of another.

One of the most disheartening things about us is the contrast between the way we mobilized for war and our blundering ineptness when it comes to mobilizing for peace.

A young man sat in my office one day and talked about his experience during the past few years. He told me that he hated most of the things about the army. But at least he was willing to put up with that and make what sacrifices were demanded of him, because he knew the enemy had to be defeated. But since the war he went on to describe how different it was. No one seemed able to tell him where we were going. Housing was impossible, and so far as he could tell, nothing was being done about it that was at all commensurate with the importance of the crisis. Facing the contrast between then and now, he told me in all seriousness that the possibility of another war did not shock him too much.

How quickly we deteriorate in times of peace. How quickly young men who swore in the midst of danger that it would be different when they came home, forget that high resolve. How easy it is to let a small reactionary group take control of an organization and speak on the reactionary side of every issue, while the bulk of the membership keeps silent. How easy it is to justify squeezing money from the public treasury.

In my own state, which I assume is no worse and no better than other states of the union, about a million bushels of corn were used in 1946 to produce hard liquor. If that is a fair average for the nation, then the United States used one hundred million bushels of corn for liquor in that year. All that needs to be said about it is that in this same year people were starving to death in Europe. A friend reported that in the railroad stations in Germany there were signs asking people not to throw food to children. Why? Because youngsters were badly hurt and some killed as they scrambled desperately for it.

The chancellor of one of our state universities, who is a first-rate scientist and worked on the development of the atom bomb, told me that the contrast between our willingness to spend money for death and our fumbling hesitancy to spend money for life appalled him. Do we want to be saved? Then we had better remove our tendency to put our small comfortable groups ahead of our concern for the world's fate.

Van Gogh, the painter who became famous after he was dead, was slow in developing his powers. He had a brother who was very interested in the boy's talent. The brother said to him one day, "I keep looking at every new sketch you make, saying to myself, 'Has he come into his maturity yet? But thus far . . .'" So God must look upon a world which the pressure of events should have made mature by this time. The signs in the skies are plain enough. "Surely," He says, "they will know now what they must do to be saved. But thus far, no!" That God could do what needs to be done whether we respond or not, I am very sure. But that He will refuse to save us until we do our part, I am certain. Social salvation awaits our willingness to remove some of our favorite sins, and it will be as difficult as taking out an eye.

The Church

The most significant factor in redeeming the times is the Church. It represents the one best hope for tomorrow, but it is also true that it can become a stumbling block to its own purpose. It is sometimes true that the Church stands in the way of fulfilling the destiny decreed for it by God. In this present time, the world may well say to the Church: "Physician, heal thyself."

The Church must get rid of its desire for popularity. In this it is not different from other institutions which have given too many hostages to the *status quo*. But if it is to be an instrument of salvation, it must root out this desire, though it be like plucking out an eye.

A religious movement tends to follow a well-defined pat-

tern. It begins as a minority, despised by the majority and
hated if it continues to grow. Such a group is not tempted
very much to seek popularity because it is not within the
possibility of attainment. The people who join such a movement are not influenced by the desire to increase their social
status. Quite the contrary, for joining the movement is
a loss of social prestige. But if the movement grows, it
gradually becomes rich and powerful. Its creativeness gives
way to a desire for standing and acceptance. To protect
and increase this desire, it begins to water down the hard
sections of its doctrine. Instead of pioneering, it follows.
Its first question is no longer: Does the Lord command it?
but, What will the influential people think? It will become
in time merely a pious genuflection. At one period in its
history, a man defined the Church of England as the Tory
Party at prayer. But this is no more true of one particular
church than it is of others. It is a part of a universal
process.

The Church I am most familiar with is my own—the
Methodist. It began with little groups of people meeting
together in "class meetings." Of them it would need to be
said as St. Paul said of the Corinthians: "that not many
wise after the flesh, not many mighty, not many noble,
are called" (I Corinthians 1:26). What those early Methodists
did for England in the eighteenth century is a matter of
history. It is not too much to say, however, that they were
a significant part in the salvation of a people. But the one
thing they were not, so far as the pillars of society were concerned, was popular.

Now it is all so different. The years have added numbers
until we are accepted as an "orthodox" denomination. The
years have brought wealth, at least in comparison with our
financial status at the beginning. We have been given influence; we have become respectable. In place of despising
popularity, now we crave it. Our steps are more sedate and

careful, and our public pronouncements tend to be more general. We are not very different from other citizens. We are not as willing to heed William Law's "Serious Call" as was John Wesley and the early Methodists. As a result, salvation is not mediated through us as it ought to be and as it could be.

We who tend to despise the strange sects of our time, need to be very careful lest we look down on people who are better instruments of God's will than are we. At least, they are not afraid to bear a witness which is not a popular one. Not many people in our congregations would go through what they go through. Not many of us are willing to risk the displeasure of our neighbors, as they do. This is not in itself a sign of truth, but it is the sign of a serious purpose in doing what is necessary to be saved.

The great creative days of any religious movement have been the days of unpopularity, and often, of persecution. The Prophets never spoke for their society as a whole. They did not say what they said with any idea that it would make them popular. Not until they were safely dead did their teaching find a place in the common faith of the people. Yet their saving influence in Israel's life was precisely their willingness to proclaim the wisdom of God which seemed to the majority then, as it does now, sheer foolishness. If the Church wants to save, it must cut out its desire for popularity.

The Church needs to pluck out its hope of being a majority. Some years ago I made a speech at a conference, in the course of which I suggested the Church ought to be a creative minority. One of my older colleagues took me aside afterward and said, "You never should hint that the Church is anything but a majority." Well, if we produce an institution that will appeal to the majority, you can be sure that it is too broad to have any cutting edge. The trouble with us now is that there are times when we have difficulty in describing any real difference between churchmen and non-churchmen.

Majorities have not had much part in shaping tomorrow. The great minorities who know where they are going and have some sense of mission, are the potent forces in a society. Salvation is not from majorities. "Not by might, nor by power, but by my Spirit, saith Jehovah of hosts" (Zechariah 4:6). John Wesley came to one of his class meetings and found that in their zeal to increase their numbers, they had lowered the requirements. He expelled a number of them and wrote in his *Journal* that they had a glorious revival.

Perhaps the Old Testament story of Gideon has a modern application for the Church. Gideon was commissioned to drive out the Midianites who had overrun the land. He sent out his call for help and thirty-two thousand men responded. His amazement must have been great when God said there were too many. Gideon released all who were a little fearful of the outcome, and twenty-two thousand went home. But God said there were still too many. You remember how Gideon was commanded to have them drink from a stream and

> everyone that lappeth of the water with his tongue, as a dog lappeth, him shalt thou set by himself; likewise everyone that boweth down upon his knees to drink. And the number of them lapped, putting their hand to their mouth, was three hundred men.   JUDGES 7:5-6

And the land was freed by three hundred men. It will not be by mere numbers that the Church will be saved or will save. We had better put more emphasis on the hard sayings of Jesus, and the cutting off of hands, if that is necessary, to be redeemed.

God is saying to the Church, "You had better pluck out your desire for ease." If we had been told fifteen years ago that the time would come very soon when Christians would be persecuted in the Christian countries of Europe, we could not have believed it. The only place where we might have thought such a thing could conceivably happen was in some superstition-ridden, ignorant land. But we have seen Christians persecuted in countries with the heritage of Western civilization, which is a Christian heritage. Was that persecution mania only a thing of one race, of one nation? No, Nazism is not just a German product, unfortunately. It is not confined to any particular geographical area. It is in the heart of mankind, and it is within our own borders.

Who shall save us from it? Our experience says that the chief obstacle to the fascist madness is the Christian Gospel. But if a Church believes that the battle is over and it is now time to take its ease, then the pagan gods of blood and soil begin to stir. A saving Church has to be one that has refused ease. A churchman is one who never yields to his desire for ignoble withdrawal from the struggle.

Surely we can hear God's voice saying to the Christian Church today, "You must get rid of your divisions and your bickerings." It is time for Christians of all groups who are aware of the crisis of the moment to think of the Church against the world. Protestantism must unite. One of the crying scandals of our time is little towns with five or six struggling churches where there ought to be only one. If there is one good thing about the march of Catholicism toward political power in America, it is that Protestantism must begin to see the necessity of unity. But it will be too bad if that conflict continues to grow. Can we not believe we belong together, and more than our differences is our common faith? The task of saving a secular society is too great for any one part of the Church. Separation is a luxury we can no longer afford. If the Church wants to be saved, it must cut off its tendency to civil war. If it would save the world, it must pluck out its sectarianism.

Remember St. Paul on his way to Rome. He was a prisoner

on board ship. Perhaps we may be allowed to use our imagination a little as we think of that voyage. We know that he warned the Centurion not to sail from the harbor at Fair Havens. But the captain did not like the harbor to winter in, and the voyage was continued. When the storm struck and the ship was in danger of going down, we can imagine that the captain remembered Paul's warning. "What shall we do now?" he asked. Paul said, "Throw the cargo over. Get rid of all the gear. Only by lightening the ship can we be saved." But the captain replied, "The cargo is the main reason for this voyage. We are taking the cargo to Rome. I cannot throw it overboard." "Would you rather lose the cargo and live," asked the Apostle, "or keep the cargo and die?" Then though it was one of the hardest things he had ever done, the captain gave the order to lighten the ship.

To the Church of Christ there comes in this hour the command to throw away some of our favorite vices. We have had them a long time and they have become precious to us. But if the Church would be saved, then saith the Lord, get rid of your desire for popularity, your hope to be a majority, your search for ease, and your sectarianism. Only by lightening the ship, can the Church save itself and this generation.

Personal Salvation

We would like to be saved but not badly enough to give up the things which stand in the way of our salvation. Is it a free gift? Yes. But the gift is always dependent not only on the giver, but also on the receiver. What does the gift of a book mean to a savage who cannot read? Of what significance is the gift of love to the person satiated with lust? Only the thirsty man will appreciate and be able to receive the cup of cold water. Life is a matter of discrimination. We cannot have everything. Until we have decided for ourselves what is the supreme value, we will clutter up

our lives with so many useless things that the precious gifts
cannot be received because there is no room for them.

We must get rid of hatred. No man can enter into life as
long as there is resentment in his heart against someone. It
will not work. But you say, "I have every reason to hate that
person and I have nursed my hatred along for so many years
that it would be like cutting off a hand to part with it."
That is just what Jesus said it would be like. But would you
rather keep your hatred and die, or give it up and live?
Many a man tries to pray, but when he lifts his petition,
there is a barrier between himself and God. My prayer cannot rise higher than my head until my personal forgiveness gives it wings.

We must cut away our pride and our arrogance. We want
to bolster up our feeling of superiority, and so we look down
at some poor fellow who has brought disgrace upon himself and his family. We say to ourselves that we are better
than he is. He stole, but we never did. He disintegrated
morally, but we have remained respectable. Let us read again
the Beatitudes. Until we can weep with those who weep,
and sympathize with those who sorrow, and share the burden
of the heavy-laden, we cannot know salvation. Before I can
be saved, I must be able to associate myself with every man
whatever his status may be and say, "There but for the
grace of God, go I."

In some ways the most difficult thing to pluck out is our
self-pity. More of us fall into this pit than into any other.
We can find a hundred excuses for not being any better than
we are. We can marshal a hundred arguments justifying
our selfish acts. We can think of a hundred reasons why we
are better than others. Can salvation find its way into our
hearts through this barrier? It cannot.

William James was once so torn by the frustrating experience of life that he seriously considered suicide. But he
came through the ordeal and wrote these words:

There is a state of mind known to religious men, but to no others, in which the will to assert one's own has been displaced by a willingness to close our mouths and be as nothing in the floods and waterspouts of God. . . . The time for tension in our soul is gone, and that of happy relaxation, of calm deep breathing, of an eternal present with no discordant future to be anxious about has arrived.

When we are willing to do the thing which Jesus said was as difficult as plucking out an eye or cutting off a hand, then we can know this peace of salvation.

A critic once accused Professor Denney of Glasgow of accepting as authentic only a dozen or so sayings of Jesus in the Gospels. He pointed out, for example, that Dr. Denney had never preached on the words of Jesus, "Come unto me." When a friend asked him about it, that fine Christian said with a broken voice: "I have never been able to." None can begin to tell what it means to be sought after and saved by Christ. But once we dimly apprehend its meaning, we shall find power to do whatever is necessary to let him have his way with us. Salvation is ours if we want it badly enough to make room for it. "Thanks be to God for his unspeakable gift" (II Corinthians 9:15).

VII

FORGIVENESS AND THE SCAPEGOAT

". . . who can forgive sins but one, even God?"

MARK 2:7

The forgiveness of sins is not a unique doctrine of Christianity. Long before the coming of Jesus, Judaism proclaimed this central religious truth. The Jews did not object

to Jesus'. teaching that God forgives sins, but they objected
to his assumption that forgiveness could come from him.
This seemed to them a blasphemy. Yet Christians have
found that in some special way God reconciles men to Himself through Christ.

The Scapegoat

It has never been easy for men to believe that they needed
forgiveness or to ask for it when they were at last convinced
of their need. We will do almost anything to escape our
sense of guilt rather than confess and ask to be forgiven.
There is a passage in the Old Testament which symbolizes
this mad attempt to throw our sins on something else. In
the ritual of atonement there is this direction:

> And when he hath made an end of atoning for the holy
> place, and the tent of meeting, and the altar, he shall present
> the live goat: and Aaron shall lay both his hands upon the
> head of the live goat, and confess over him all the iniquities
> of the children of Israel, and all their transgressions, even all
> their sins; and he shall put them upon the head of the goat,
> and shall send him away by the hand of a man that is in
> readiness into the wilderness: and the goat shall bear upon
> him all their iniquities unto a solitary land: and he shall
> let go the goat in the wilderness.   LEVITICUS 16:20-22

Long before this happened and ever since it happened there
has been a terrible fascination in the idea of a scapegoat.
We want to pour our sins on something or someone and
send them into the wilderness never to return to bother us.

The doctrine of the Atonement has often been presented
in just this light. Jesus on the Cross is regarded as a sort
of divine scapegoat. By repeating a few words in a creed
men think they can be freed of their guilt and responsibility.
It is no wonder that the very sound of "blood" in connection
with Christianity has an unreal, sentimental connotation
for many modern Christians. It has been associated with
ideas repugnant to men who have some understanding of
the enormity of sin and its consequences, and have ideas

of God beyond the mechanical, infantile stage. It is not so easy to get rid of sin. It takes more than passing it on to Christ orally.

In the political area there is a tendency to find a scapegoat rather than to confess national guilt and seek an ultimate remedy. Back of the debacle of Germany there was fundamental dishonesty when it came to facing national problems. There are not many who would claim that the Versaille Treaty was what it ought to have been. It was full of injustices and stupidities. Quite so! But it became for the German people a scapegoat on which they could lay all their troubles. Even for many of Germany's former enemies it stood as the chief reason for the world's troubles. The Treaty was driven into the wilderness, but it was not able to carry all the sins of the world.

Today, the Western democracies are doing the same thing with the communists. There is just enough truth in the idea of their guilt to make it possible to blame everything on them. But more important than shouting about communism's obvious evils and its constant heckling of our efforts toward reconstruction, is an honest effort to set our own house in order. But that is most difficult and demands giving up many things we want to keep. In the thinking of too many people the crucifixion of communism would be an adequate atonement for democracy.

The social order is always seeking a whipping boy, and he is never too hard to find. Once it was the Christians who were chosen for the role, and Nero heaped the sins of Rome on them and they were sent into a flaming wilderness. Most of the Protestant denominations played that part in the beginning, as the Methodists did in England. Too often the most convenient whipping boy is the Jew, and if business is bad or we need to compensate for a feeling of inferiority, we drive him into exile. Foreigners of any kind are natural victims of this impulse. If you are in a state of war, then you can drive from the West Coast the American-Japanese and feel virtuous about it while you take their property at a sacrifice and get rid of troublesome agricultural competition.

Groups hurl their accusations against their rivals and try to persuade the public that everything wrong should be laid on their backs. The party out of power can show how all the ills are due to the party in power, who in turn can show that they inherited them from the party now out of power. Business is sure that the fault is labor's and if unions are stripped of all their evil practices, all will be well. Labor replies that the real villain is management. All who are nostalgic for the good old days tell us with great seriousness that the country is full of agitators, and they are the real scapegoats.

This is a universal, human tendency. John Gunther said that after touring the South he came to the conclusion that one of its greatest problems is the number of southerners whose only profession is being southerners. They are not the only ones who have clung to a romantic, unrealistic picture of the past rather than deal with the obvious evils of the present. One of the men I have known best in my lifetime, was a man who never blamed himself for his mistakes and his failures. It was always that the breaks were against him, or he was betrayed by a man or a circumstance. Of him it could have been said, "This man might have been saved if just once he had confessed he had sinned and was to blame."

The trouble with this scapegoat fascination is that it solves nothing and finally destroys us. It simply postpones the inevitable tragedy. Psychoanalysis has revealed how pretense in this field leads to twisted, ruined lives. Each man has to face his own sin, and if he cannot bear to look at it, then it will haunt him like a black ghost until he cracks. How many people are guilt-haunted! The time comes when all the guilt which we have tried to send away by the scapegoat through the years, suddenly descends upon our spirits like a thick fog. The only thing that will dispel that fog and lift that fear, is an act of God.

Forgiveness

Great religion is not born out of fear of punishment, but out of love for the God

> Who forgiveth all thine iniquities;
> Who healeth all thy diseases;
> Who redeemeth thy life from destruction;
> Who crowneth thee with lovingkindness and tender mercies . . .   PSALM 103:3-4

One of the earliest and greatest witnesses of this experience of forgiveness from God through Christ was St. Paul. Those who have tried to make him a theologian moving in the realm of abstract ideas have done him more harm than Alexander the Coppersmith. Many a theory of the Atonement has come from the writings of Paul, and by taking passages out of the context, you can find almost anything you look for. But underneath everything else, Paul is bearing witness to the experience of being forgiven and set free from the domination of sin. As the slave was sometimes released from bondage and given his freedom by being ritualistically purchased by a god, so Paul became free by becoming a slave of Christ. It was not only that God in Christ had done something for Paul, but that he had done something *to* him. Forgiveness changed his life.

The Greek Fathers were aware of sin as a corruption of human nature. Somehow, they believed, through God becoming flesh in Jesus, the power of sin was broken. It was in the nature of a transaction and at its worst this thought suggested that God had to pay a ransom to the Devil in order to make the forgiveness of man possible. That ransom, they said, was the death of His Son. Not many of us will be convinced or helped by theories such as this.

The Latin Fathers tended to think in terms of government and laws. Now and again there is a helpful insight, but too often, the theologians have been guilty of putting a great spiritual experience in the narrow confines of a mechanical explanation. The Older Protestant Theologians sometimes made the death of Christ all important and his life a mere gesture. Whenever they tried to think in terms of legal justice only, they came out with one side of a truth that was, in some ways, more misleading than a lie.

George Herbert was aware of the inadequacy of philosophical explanations of religious experiences. He wrote:

> Philosophers have measured mountains,
> Fathomed the depths of seas, of states, and kings,
> Walked with a staffe to heav'n, and traced fountains:
> But there are two vast, spacious things,
> The which to measure it doth more behove:
> Yet few there are that found them: Sinne and Love.

Men who have taken no easy viewpoint of sin cannot be satisfied with what seems an easy, sentimental view of forgiveness. That is why the rugged thinkers of yesterday sometimes leaned over backward in portraying the horror of sin when looked at from the viewpoint of God. Not for them was He an easygoing, slightly senile old man. Like Moses, they heard him thunder from Sinai. Like Isaiah, they cried out in agony when they saw their own lives in the light of His holiness. Like Jesus and Paul, they had an austere concept of God. Whatever the experience of forgiveness from such a God might be, it was not to be taken lightly. It was a terrible thing to contemplate, and a revolutionary thing to accept.

Andrew Bonar and Robert M'Cheyne were having one of their frequent walks together, talking over the ways of their ministry. "M'Cheyne asked me," said Bonar, "what my last Sabbath's subject had been. It had been: 'the wicked shall be turned into hell.' On hearing this awful text, he asked:

'Were you able to preach it with tenderness?' " And that is
the heart of the difficulty. To know of God's justice and
hatred of evil and to account for His willingness, yes, His
eagerness, to remove our guilt, "as far as the east is from the
west," is beyond our power to adequately express.

What It Does

When a man quits running away from himself and stops
pretending that his sin can be blamed on someone else,
then God has His chance to forgive him. It seems to me that
the first great part of that experience is being cleansed. To
put it on a very low level, it is like coming from the long
day's work, weary, sticky, hot, and dirty, to stand under a
cool shower.

Sin is not a gallant marching thing in the soul. It is drab-
ness and dirt. The late Archbishop of Canterbury, William
Temple, said that he heard the famous evangelist, Dr. Torrey preach in the city hall at Oxford. The thing he remembered most clearly about the sermon was that Torrey had
described his sins marching past him in the night in a scarlet
procession. Bishop Temple said, "I never feel that way; my
sins are gray, all gray." That is the general experience. Sin
takes the freshness of life away and covers the soul with a
layer of dust. It dirties everything it touches. All the cover-
ing up we do is like adding some strong, cheap perfume to
hide the fact of our uncleanness. Yet nothing is changed and
nothing is right. If only we dared to believe that it is no
longer necessary to cover things up, but that we could be
cleansed, we would become new creatures.

We cannot adjust ourselves to the idea that filth is something to get accustomed to. We cannot endure it. Because
the soul is made by God, it is made for purity and it can
never be satisfied until it is clean. That is one of those
terrible things about being human. We must be clean within.
But if we fail to find cleansing, we will live like fugitives

fleeing from the real and imagined fears created by our guilt.

Forgiveness is cleansing. The joy of being converted is the joy of losing the stains of our sin. The more a man has been aware of this need, the greater his glorying in the forgiveness of God. Paul writes:

> Now the works of the flesh are manifest, which are these: fornication, uncleanness, lasciviousness, idolatry, sorcery, enmities, strife, jealousies, wraths, factions, divisions, parties, envyings, drunkenness, revellings, and such like; of which I forewarn you even as I did forewarn you, that they who practice such things shall not inherit the kingdom of God.
>
> GALATIANS 5:19-21

Our own consciences forewarn us of that. In our own best moments we know we cannot live until we have been made clean.

The source of our words and actions is our inner, secret life and it puts its mark on every word spoken and every action consummated. Can a harlot speak of love without dirtying the word? What does the concept of honesty mean when it is spoken by a thief? How does a traitor dare speak of patriotism? Even the truth coming from a liar has his mark on it. The forgiveness of God is the cleansing of the source of all our motives and all our acts.

Forgiveness means a new start. Chesterton said that if he were drowning, he would rather meet a burglar who could swim, than a bishop who could not. So when we are standing in the way of the flood of our guilt and uncleanness, it will not help us to have a few pious platitudes thrown our way. We must be found by someone who "sitteth upon the flood" and controls it. Out of that experience, we are reborn. Life gets a new beginning.

Whenever we are in wrong relation, we cannot start new until we have sought and obtained the forgiveness for our sins. The husband who has wronged his wife may

decide to let bygones be bygones and try to do better in the
future. But until he has confessed his wrong and obtained
her forgiveness, there is no new start. There is only the old
relationship poisoned constantly by a festering sense of un-
forgiven wrong. And there must be on the wife's part a
willingness to forgive. It won't work if it is like the husband
who said to his wife after a quarrel, "I thought you had
agreed to forgive and forget." She replied: "Sure, but I don't
want you to forget that I have forgiven and forgotten."[1]
God's promise is that our transgressions are blotted out of all
remembrance.

There is no way for any man to escape his past. We reap
what we have sown and we suffer for our sin. But the trans-
forming power of Christ takes all these hangovers from the
past and somehow rearranges them. The pattern is different.
The future is different. "Behold, I make all things new,"
saith the Lord.

The psychological word for this experience of forgiveness
is integration. We cease being at war with ourselves and become unified persons made whole by His divine act upon
our spirits. It is a human necessity to find a true center
around which we can organize our lives. The tragedy for
many a man is that he finds nothing but a cheap substitute
for this thing he needs. It is pathetic to observe the number of people who vaguely grope for something around
which their vagrant longings may be organized. They know
that something is wrong and cannot be right until they find
the center. So great is this need for integration, that people
are tempted to force it on too low a level.

Lewis Browne's *See What I Mean?* is the story of a demagogue. One of the characters describes him in these words:

> Right from the start I suspected that deep down he was
> fundamentally nuts. What's more even though I'm no long-
> haired professor of psychology, I managed to figure out just

[1] Smith, *This Love of Ours,* Abingdon-Cokesbury, 1947.

what he was nuts about. Fundamentally, I mean. It wasn't the Jews. The more I studied him the surer I became that his Jew-complex wasn't basic at all. He knocked them only because he wanted to boost something else. And do you know what that something else was? I'll tell you. It was himself . . . John Christian Power was in the strict literal sense just crazy about himself.[2]

The sad truth is that too many of us have been unable to find anything higher or finer to build around than ourselves.

In contrast, there is the experience of Robert Barclay who attended the meetings of the Quakers in the early period of their life when there was much hostility raised against them. He said:

When I came into the silent assemblies of God's people, I felt a secret power among them, which touched my heart, and I gave way unto it. I found the evil weakening in me and the good raised up; and thus I became knit and united unto them, hungering more and more after the increase of this power and life.

What a difference there is here! Over against the madness of egocentricity there is the power and peace of God. To be forgiven, is to be integrated on the only truly human level, which is on His level.

Forgiveness is the prerequisite for the creation of the humble heart. A man who has not been confronted with his sin and then experienced its forgiveness can hardly know the joy of the humble. Bennett Cerf tells about an overpublicized author who had submitted to a mass interview. After it was over, one of the interviewers remarked to another, "He isn't quite as conceited as I'd been led to expect." "Ah, yes," added another, "but he has so much to be modest about." So have we all, but it is not easy to be modest. It is too easy to be proud.

The great souls have had their pride washed away. In

[2] Browne, *See What I Mean?* Random House, 1943.

them there is depth and power. The surface storms seem to leave their spirits untroubled. They are like the men who have escaped death by a hair's breadth and spend their remaining years in a constant thanksgiving for the gift of life which they feel they do not deserve. They are like men who have loved in what they thought must be a hopeless fashion, but have had their love returned. They can never get over this miracle that has happened to them. They are, in a word, the men whose sins have been forgiven and they are forever trying to find a way to express their thanks.

The Apostle Paul has this quality of humility. He writes:

> Unto me, who am less than the least of all saints, was this grace given, to preach unto the Gentiles the unsearchable riches of Christ.   EPHESIANS 3:8

It is the picture of a man standing in amazement before an experience too wonderful to believe. This is the attitude of the saints of all ages. They preach "the unsearchable riches of Christ" and it is too great an honor to be taken easily.

No one can come anywhere near expressing the truth in the Christian experience of forgiveness. But the difficulty of the definition is a sign of its profundity. Precisely because we cannot explain it, we know it is something fundamental. The reason we fumble when we try to define its meaning is because there is nothing with which we can compare it. No one ever had anything happen to him like the forgiveness of God. But we can say that the testimony of Christians is that it cleanses, it provides a new beginning, it integrates, and it fills us with the joy of humility.

Human Response

In one of the times when I was most confused, a teacher said to me that if one is having difficulty in finding God, he should begin with his personal relations. He went on to suggest that this is where God finds men and this is often the place where we find God. The truth is that the key to Christian revelation is in personal dealings, one with another. Until we have brought our religious ideas into the realm of relationships, they remain academic and unreal.

No place is this more apparent than when we are talking about forgiveness. It is stated specifically in the New Testament that God's forgiveness is not possible without our willingness to forgive. At least once a week, most Christians repeat the Lord's Prayer. Nothing could be plainer than the words: "Forgive us our trespasses, as we forgive those who trespass against us." How do we dare to pray this prayer? The answer is that most of us do not give it a thought. We repeat so many rhythmical words without stopping to consider their meaning. It might well be that some of us would not have the courage to pray the Lord's Prayer if we thought it through. Certainly to consider it seriously will demand radical changes on the part of us all.

On the basis of this prayer, we have little right to claim God's forgiveness unless we have accepted our obligation to be forgiving. The unforgiving spirit has canceled out its claim for pardon. The hate-filled heart does not deserve the love of God. The bitter seeker after revenge has made his choice. If he obtains his revenge, it may seem very sweet to him. But he can never know the joy of God's forgiveness. He cannot have it both ways.

To some, this seems like a vindictive spirit. Why shouldn't God forgive us whether we reciprocate or not? What kind of love is it that measures itself out only as it is deserved? Edgar Lee Masters in a novel of some years past attacks this idea of forgiveness as belonging to the gods of revenge and hate. It is a human thing to want something for nothing.

Even when we deny the right of others to make such a claim on us, we would like to make such a claim on God.

But what these critics miss is something that is obvious to the explorers of the spiritual world. It is simply that God does not withhold His mercy from us to repay us for being unmerciful, but His mercy cannot enter our lives past the barrier of our hardness. The spiritual world has its laws too. Hatred builds a barrier between my soul and God, and He cannot, at least He will not, override it.

If God would treat us as servants or slaves, it would be quite different. If He would act as a King and command His subjects, we would not be troubled with the problem of our reaction. But as long as we are friends, then the relationship can only be preserved by free response. If we are His sons, then until we adjust our lives to what sonship demands, the Father must wait to bestow on us His gifts.

How limited are the powers of a father to give his son all that he would like to give him. Can he give him character? Only the inspiration for it! The hard achievement must be the boy's responsibility. Can he give him a college education? He may provide funds for it, but the education itself is only possible when the boy wants it and works for it. Can a father make his son a success in a profession? No, he can give him every encouragement and surround him with temptations to do the right thing. But the response is always the boy's. We know that our own character is not an adequate defense against the evil of the world. We know that God stands ready to be our defense. But without our response, He must wait. To fling ourselves on His mercy, means to make room for Him in our hearts.

Our God is at once succor and a consuming fire. To help us, He will burn out the self-centeredness and the evil. To be the recipients of His grace and forgiveness is to be shaken from our complacency and aroused from the comfortable acceptance of our sin. For the Jews, it meant suffering and wandering. For Jeremiah, it was a call to a task so repugnant that he cursed the day of his birth. For Jesus, the path led to the Cross. For Paul, it was shipwreck, beatings and martyrdom. Does any man think we can take His forgiveness without effort? If we are to be forgiven, then He will insist that we let Him burn out our unforgiving tendencies.

There was a British chaplain who said to his men: "Don't you chaps get the idea that God is a bloody fool." The language is strong but the situation no doubt demanded it. There are too many people telling us (and we are easy to convince) that God can cure us painlessly and without any effort on our part. We are in need of purging, for we have done so much evil. As the converted sinner in John Masefield's poem said, "The harm I done being me." Because the disease is serious, the healing cannot always be gentle.

Dr. Harry Holmes says that a Persian was explaining to an Englishman how Persian rugs are made. He described how the frame is set up and how boys on one side put through the threads as they are directed by the artist from the opposite side. The Englishman asked: "What happens if a boy makes a mistake?" "Oh," said the Persian, "often he never knows about it. For the artist quickly changes the design to compensate for the error. When the rug is finished, no one can tell where the mistake was made."

Is that not a parable of God and His forgiveness? Because we are men, we are not perfect. None of us is wise enough to keep from blunders and wrong choices. But the man whose heart has been filled with God's love and forgiveness, finds the design of his life is adjusted to compensate for his sin. Forgiveness does not wipe out the past. It does more than that. It brings all of life, including its blunders, into God's purposes, which is to say, it saves us.

VIII

THE HALF-WITTED BROTHER

> *"My God . . . why hast thou forsaken me?"*
>
> MARK 15:34

W. Macneile Dixon in his fine book, *The Human Situation*, says a traveler reported the philosophy of an African tribe in these words: "They said that although God is good, and wishes good for everybody, unfortunately he has a half-witted brother, who is always interfering with what he does. This half-witted brother keeps obtruding himself and does not give God a chance."[1] I do not suppose there is a people anywhere whose greatest thinkers have not wrestled with this problem of evil. There is not a man willing to think of life seriously, who is not forced to struggle with this mystery. Even those who have not consciously sat down to spin a theory about suffering, have unconsciously accepted some view of it. No way of life dares to leave it out.

Christianity has a word to speak concerning the "half-witted brother." It meets the problem head on with its usual realistic manner. One of its chief claims to our allegiance is the way it deals with suffering. It has a positive word about the meaning of pain. It has an answer—not neatly done up in a little package, but big and rugged. The Christian answer comes from the experience of many centuries and from many testimonies.

One of the first gropings for a religious solution to the

[1] Dixon, *The Human Situation*, Longman's, Green, 1938.

problem is found in the Old Testament. It is rather simple, and for some people it is still quite satisfying. It is, in a word, that suffering means sin. This view holds that when a person suffers, he is being branded by God as a sinner. If all the time he has seemed a good man to his neighbors, it only means that he has been a secret sinner and God has at last caught up with him. I say this is satisfying to some people—especially to those who are not suffering themselves.

This idea has been popular because it contains some truth. There is a real connection between sin and pain. Evil does bring suffering. The universe is moral and we have learned to expect that punishment will follow guilt. To a people who had no doctrine of personal immortality, it was almost inevitable that this idea should flourish. For in their scheme, whatever punishment or reward a man was going to receive, he had to receive here and now. In the after existence, everybody was the same. Suffering as punishment for sin was so satisfying and so neat.

Today there are many who still hold to this belief in slightly modified form. The successful man has a hard time in not believing that his success is a well-earned reward for his virtue. He knows that he has worked long and hard. The pressure of his obligations has made it impossible for him to do much carousing, even if he were so inclined. He notes also that failure often is due to laziness. He cannot see why any man willing to live industriously, as he has done, cannot achieve the wealth and the success he has achieved.

We in America have something of this belief. We think the starvation and suffering of European nations must be the result of their badness. At least nothing like that has happened to us. Why don't they behave themselves? We must be better than all the rest. We won, didn't we? It is the easiest thing in the world to see in our success God's reward for better behavior.

Yet this belief has obvious objections. Job stated most of them a long time ago. He said that sometimes the good suffer even more than the wicked. There seems to be no assurance that goodness will escape pain. When an earthquake strikes or a flood comes, there seems to be a curious lack of discrimination. Whoever stands in the way of it, suffers the onslaught. But even worse that that, success so often means the death of virtues, instead of their development. It is sometimes true that whom the gods would destroy, they first make too successful. What the world calls success, at least, is often a judgment of God.

The world of human experience will not yield to any of our mechanistic theories. The natural world has its laws and its dependabilities, but in the realm of human experience, we cannot establish our science. Something is always disproving our best laid plans. We must be suspicious of all simple solutions. And this idea is too simple and too logical. It will not fit all the facts. It will not answer all the questions which demand an answer.

Another simple solution of the problem is to regard evil as illusory. We may think it exists, says this theory, but it does not. It is error. If we can get hold of our thoughts and keep them in the straight and narrow way, we shall be able to live free from pain. This idea, like the previous one, has some truth in it. No one can deny that thinking has a great deal to do with suffering. The mind has powers of healing over the body. "For as he thinketh within himself, so is he" (Proverbs 23:7). Anyone who reads his Bible knows that healing the sick by faith and prayer is good orthodox Christianity.

It has been said that no one gets a great idea without carrying it too far. That many a person needs to learn how to think health, most of us would agree. Sickness for many people is in the mind. To carry this idea of the illusory nature of evil to its extreme, however, makes it ridiculous, and certainly makes it non-Christian. To draw the inference that all sickness is illusion, simply does not stand up under very close scrutiny.

If it should be that suffering is an illusion, then the illusion would appear to be an evil. For certainly most people are the victims of the illusion. Are men to be regarded as such dupes as this? Did not Jesus suffer? When it seemed that even God had deserted him, was the experience an illusion? Is the Cross only a symbol of something that does not really exist? We cannot believe it. The evidence will not support it.

This bit of doggerel contains a valid criticism:

> There was a faith healer of Deal,
> Who said, "Although pain isn't real,
> When I sit on a pin,
> And it punctures my skin,
> I dislike what I fancy I feel.

However we may explain it, there is something in the human situation which leads us through the valley of the shadow. The most universal fellowship of all is the fellowship of those who have known pain.

Another belief that has been popular is that evil is merely the servant of the good. In some strange way, which is not always apparent, this theory insists that what seems to be bad, is serving the purposes of righteousness. Even when we cannot see the possible connection between the two, those who take this position say that this is due to our ignorance, and in heaven we shall understand. St. Paul said, "And we know that to them that love God all things work together for good, even to them that are called according to his purpose" (Romans 8:28). But this is something different. The Apostle is speaking of people who have surrendered completely to God. He is not saying that evil always works for good. Nor would he intimate that a Christian will not know pain.

This belief is usually held by comfortable people, which, in itself, tells us something about it. It is a rather easy thing to think that what is happening to someone else will eventually work out for the best. My friend Elton Trueblood quoted some lines in one of his books which sums this up:

> The toad beneath the harrow knows
> Exactly where each tooth-point goes;
> The butterfly, upon the road,
> Preaches contentment to the toad.[2]

L. P. Jacks saw the whole difficulty clearly when he said:

> I read the other day a book intended to justify the ways of God to man, which argued that if men are to have teeth at all they must have teeth that can ache. There must therefore be such a thing as a toothache. Quite so. But what if the number of aching teeth in the world at this moment is a hundred times as great as it need be? And why should the aching be as violent as it is? Would not a milder and more endurable form of the malady satisfy the requirements of the argument? And why should my teeth ache rather than yours?[3]

That there may be hints of truth in these and other explanations, most of us would agree. But that we have in any of them an answer that is satifying to men who are suffering, is not true. We shall not expect to discover the ultimate probing of the mystery of suffering. But we need more than these facile explanations. We need enough light shining into the darkness of pain to help us bear it. For that, we must turn to the Gospel. It has the most profound understanding of the problem.

God's Limitations

In the first place, we are face to face with a God who has certain self-limitations. I do not mean what Professor

[2] Trueblood, *The Logic of Belief,* Harper, 1942, 289. This book contains one of the best discussions of suffering.

[3] *Ibid.,* 289, from Jacks, *Religious Foundations,* 103.

William Pepperell Montague means by his teaching of the limitations of God. He says that either God is all-powerful and bad, or else He is good, but not all-powerful. No one, Professor Montague believes, can look at our tragic world and believe that a good God would allow these conditions to exist if He were able to prevent them. The only answer is, therefore, that He cannot prevent them.

There is a sense in which it is true that He cannot prevent suffering. But the answer is in the realm of God's inability to contradict Himself and His own long purposes. Freedom always puts limitations on the use of power. If a ruler believes that freedom of his people is more precious than having his own way, he must limit himself in the use of power. Yet he may be able to force his way if he chooses. He is limited not because he is weak, but because he is strong enough to keep his sense of values straight.

Let us put it in another way. A father knows what is best for his children. He has been over the path they have yet to travel and he knows what lies ahead. He can exercise his authority and force them to obey his will. In that case, they will not make some of the mistakes they will otherwise make. But neither will they achieve experience and wisdom. An outsider might say to this man, "If you were the master of the situation, why didn't you prevent your boy from hurting himself as he did? How can you justify letting your daughter go through that terrible experience?" But what could the father answer? He would have to say that the most difficult thing for him was to have the authority to make his children do his will, but not use that authority. Only because he knew that freedom alone could produce character in his children and authority would prove to be self-defeating, could he find strength to limit his use of power.

In the days of war, how many times have people cried out in agony: If God can prevent this and if He is good, why does He allow it to go on? He allowed it to go on because we brought it about, and to save us from the consequences of our folly, would mean the destruction of the moral order of the universe. Could God prevent the war? I think so. But could man ever learn how to be free if God stepped in whenever things became tragic and wiped out the results of his sin? I think not.

God is not a dictator. He is not even a benevolent despot. He is a Father. There are accidents which men suffer, and perhaps if their lives had been regimented, they would not have suffered them. There is pain that comes from blunders and from upheavals of nature. The innocent suffer for the guilty. We are so bound together that what effects one will effect us all. Each man bears the responsibility for every other man, and each man, in a sense, bears the sins of all the world. All of these things speak to us of the limitations of God, but the limitations are the signs of His power.

There is a rough analogy in the difference between a democracy and a totalitarian state. Certain it is that there are some things which go on in a democracy, no self-respecting tyrant would put up with for five minutes. There may be less efficiency and more waste. There is more debating and slower action, sometimes when the issue is vital. But the regimented man who is the product of the closed system is something different from the free man who is the foundation of a democracy. A dictator, compared to an elected head of a free people responsible to the people, seems to be many times more powerful. In a sense he is, but in another sense he is not. The limitation of power is not always weakness. Sometimes it is strength.

A man asked Peter Green one time how he could preach of a God who loved men while a war was going on. Peter Green said, "You are very hard on God. Just fancy you are God and tell us what you would do. You must not say you would not allow sin, for that is to destroy man's character as a free being. But what else would you do?" The man thought for a while and then he said, "I would not let anyone suffer for anyone's fault but his own." And Peter Green said: "What a dreadful world that would be. What do you propose to do with mothers? I suppose when her son comes to the gallows, or her daughter to shame, mother is to go laughing down the street saying, 'I don't care. It does not trouble me.' The world would be one without parents, friends, saints or heroes."

Purpose of God

For another thing, through the eyes of Christ we see something of God's purpose. It becomes fairly obvious that His chief purpose is not that men should be happy. In spite of the popularity of that philosophy in our time, there is no indication in the Bible or in the world of human experience that this is His ultimate aim. It may be the desire of certain individuals for themselves, but God seems to have something beyond that in mind.

Neither is the world a reflection of the plans of one who wants us to live in a Garden of Eden. The age of innocency is over. The world is not an environment for angels and it does not put a premium on softness. It demands courage, but most of all it demands faith. Life is constantly forcing us out as it did Abraham to a land we know not. The safety which so many people long for, is not possible in this world. It is a training ground for character. If it has any purpose at all, it is to create free personalities.

We cannot make life a moral slot machine. We cannot put in our nickel's worth of virtue and take out our nickel's worth of reward. We can have no guarantee that virtue will pay us a dividend. To fulfill these purposes, there must be a world of risk and danger. It must be a place where there is always the possibility of tragedy and accident. Yet this does not spell purposelessness and a poor, weak God who cannot cope with things. It proclaims the reality of a God who was the Father of our Lord Jesus Christ. It speaks of love too great and too profound to eliminate suffering from the world.

One of the things we Americans can be least proud of, is the conduct of the Sacco-Vanzetti trial. At the end of the long ordeal, when both had been sentenced to death, Vanzetti made his eloquent statement:

> Now we are not a failure. . . . Never in our full life could we do such work for tolerance, for justice, for man's understanding of man as now we do by an accident. Our words—our lives—our pains—nothing! The taking of our lives—lives of a good shoemaker and a poor fish-peddler—all! That last moment belongs to us—that agony is our triumph.

He felt something beyond the reach of a miscarriage of justice. So beyond the suffering of men, there is the mark of a mighty purpose. It is a suffering world, but it is not a meaningless world.

That which is most destructive about suffering is the feeling that it is useless because it means nothing. It does not seem to fit in with any possible sense. This may be true of individual instances. Just because a man hurts himself in a particular moment does not mean necessarily that this was foreordained from the beginning to teach him some great lesson. We must confess that there are individual cases of suffering that seem to have no reason, or at least, no strict justice in their meaning. We are driven to take the longer look and to observe from within the greater framework. If someone objects that there is no reason this thing should have happened to him rather than to me, I must agree. At least from the human point of view, we can discover no reason.

But the fact that this is a world where suffering takes place means something about God and His purpose. It means something about the world and its nature. It means something about the kind of creature I am. A perfectly safe world could never produce human greatness. When one begins to think of heroes who have inspired the race, almost always they are people unconquered by suffering. One cannot think of great persons without thinking of pain. How could God provide an environment for this kind of creation, without having it a place where the innocent suffer as well as the guilty? Yet let us not carry this too far. It is a world of law, and suffering is often the result of either the willful or ignorant breaking of a law.

Tennyson wrote *The Charge of the Light Brigade* to glorify military discipline. What he really did was to reveal the stupidity of much military glory. Why should anyone in his right mind follow orders that will lead to his certain death, when he knows that the orders are a mistake? And worst of all, why should he feel noble and heroic because he does it? It is a question like this that comes to men who see suffering as only some horrible blunder. For people to take it with resignation, seems to them the height of stupidity. The only possible reaction would seem to be a screaming defiance.

But when one has accepted Jesus Christ as his truth, suffering is not just a blunder. It is the necessary risk to be taken for the fulfillment of the higher purpose of God. Some years ago a hurricane destroyed a little church on the coast of England. The people found themselves unable to replace it and made provisions to worship elsewhere. But one day a representative of the British Admiralty called on the minister to inquire when the church with its steeple was to be rebuilt. He was told of the situation. "Then," said he, "we will build it for you. That spire is on all our charts. Ships steer their courses by it." So it is that when the sea is rough and dangerous, the Christian keeps his eye on Jesus Christ. He is kept aware of his personal location and status. He can endure the storm of pain, for he is not lost in the despair of futility.

Suffering of God

But the unique contribution of Christianity to this whole problem, and the key to its deepest meaning, is its doctrine of the suffering God. Here is something so overwhelming that we have difficulty in adjusting ourselves to it. The philosopher may talk about the "unmoved mover" or the "trend." Jesus talks about the Father. The problem can never be satisfactorily faced if there is a gap between men and God. But if there is no agony to compare with His, and if we are never so sure of His close presence as when we know pain, that makes all the difference in the world.

When a father, just before administering punishment to his son, comes out with the old cliché, "This is going to hurt me more than it does you," the son resents the cliché almost as much as he does the punishment. It happens, however, that the statement is true. Possibly it is better not to say it, but parents know a hurt too great for words, when it is necessary to punish a child. Here is the experience of God on the human level.

Not everything that happens on this earth is according to His will. He does not have His way in everything. The tragic accidents are more tragic to Him than they are to us. He who wept over the city and felt compassion for the multitude, revealed the suffering of God. What other word of comfort can compare with this? We who minister to people in the hours of their bereavements, find that our best word is simply: God suffers. It was this experience that kept Israel loyal to Him, more than anything else.

Back of all our attempts to explain the Cross, there is a deep feeling that it is the symbol of a suffering God. To some, this will seem like an oversimplification, especially when one has read all the theories of the Atonement. Yet the theories are all trying to express an experience too deep and wonderful for words. The Cross has redeemed the suffering of mankind. It means that out of the worst, there comes the best. It means that nothing can separate us from the love of God. It means that no man suffers alone.

The terrible fascination of the Cross is its answer to the unsolved problems of human tragedy. We had better let it stand stark and rugged against the horizons of our minds. What a great thing it is that our faith begins with the worst and not with the best! How wonderful that the symbol of our religion is a symbol of defeat and not of victory! It is rough hewn, like life itself. It speaks of struggle. But when His light shines on it, it is the symbol of victory through defeat, and of truth which puts our little logic to shame. It is in a word, the sign of the one thing we must believe or die—that God is profoundly concerned with our redemption.

Georgia Harkness says it in "The Agony of God":

> I listened to the agony of God—
> I who am fed,
> Who never yet went hungry for a day.
> I see the dead—
> The children starved for lack of bread—
> I see, and try to pray.
>
> I listen to the agony of God—
> I who am warm,
> Who never yet have lacked a sheltering home.
> In dull alarm
> The dispossessed of hut and farm
> Aimless and "transient" roam.
>
> I listen to the agony of God—
> I who am strong,
> With health, and love, and laughter in my soul.
> I see a throng
> Of stunted children reared in wrong,
> And wish to make them whole.

> I listen to the agony of God—
> But know full well
> That not until I share their bitter cry—
> Earth's pain and hell—
> Can God within my spirit dwell
> To bring His kingdom nigh.[4]

No Final Defeat

The Gospel gives men the power of creative adjustment to the defeats of life. It does not promise special protection or special treatment. This concept of Christianity as a magical protection against the arrows of fortune, is sheer superstition. A little girl was told about God dwelling within her. Her question was, "If God is in me, why can't I do tricks?" Too many people hold to that idea. They can find comfort in special instances where a good man seems to have been miraculously protected, while a bad man received his just punishment. But the trouble with that approach is that there are too many cases where just the opposite happens. A chaplain said he had more admiration for a man who swore before he went into the danger of the battle, than he had for a Christian who pleaded for special consideration.

What, then, does the Gospel provide in the way of defense? We see it when we contrast the Stoic way and the Christian way. There is much about the Stoic that is admirable. He holds to his post though he die. He is loyal to his duty, even if he be slain. But the difficulty is that most of us are not up to it. We are not sure that we are made of the stuff of heroes. As a matter of fact, we have had a few terrible frights that made us suspect we were cowards. What about us?

For us, there are the everlasting arms. If we are cut off in this direction, God will show us another way. If we

---

[4] From *The Glory of God* by Georgia Harkness. Used by permission of the publisher, Abingdon-Cokesbury Press.

have no courage, He will provide us with courage. If we come to the place where we cannot endure it any longer, then He will step in. This is the faith of the Christian which lets him face the future without fear. It is the testimony of all who have thrown themselves on His protection and claimed His strength. How sick and cheap appear the magical interpretations of Christianity when they are compared with this eternal miracle.

One of the great passages in the Bible is Isaiah's testimony:

> . . . but they that wait for Jehovah shall renew their strength; they shall mount up with wings as eagles; they shall run, and not be weary; they shall walk, and not faint.
>
> ISAIAH 40:31

Quite deliberately, I believe, the Prophet saves the main point until the last. It is this having to walk and not faint that demands power outside ourselves. The best gift of God is the redeeming of these dreary days. Many a man who can face the sudden crisis and the spectacular disaster, cannot endure the test of having to plod wearily through dull monotony.

One of the reasons for the great appeal of the movies, is that everything is made dramatic. In the movies, men do not work week after week, but only for a few seconds. The man stricken with blindness still gets the girl. The man who loses the girl, is noble and heroic. Happiness has no chance to go stale. Suffering is dramatic and noble. And people who know dull, aching suffering, find relief for an hour in a world where grief does not last too long.

It is for all of us who must walk and not faint that Christ brings power. I shall not forget a visit with one of the finest women I have even known. She was always cheerful, but this time she was obviously troubled. She came to tell me she had just been informed by her doctor that she had an incurable cancer and not more than six months to

live. That would be enough to trouble anyone, but she
came to ask the best way of breaking the news to her family
and her friends. There was not one slightest indication that
she was concerned about herself. I found myself saying,
"This does work. If Christians cannot escape suffering, they
know how to master it." Remember the words of the Lord
Jesus, how he said, "In the world ye have tribulation: but
be of good cheer; I have overcome the world" (John 16:33).
Thus is the Christian armed against the "half-witted
brother." Thus is the Christian mind made victor over
suffering.

IX

DEMAND FOR FELLOWSHIP

*"They, therefore, being brought on
their way by the church . . ."*

ACTS 15:3

One of the most hopeful things about our present situation is the disillusionment suffered by thinking men. The
return to paganism has not worked out too well, and many
who leaned in that direction secretly are no longer enthusi-
astic. Our time has in this respect resembled the fourth
century and the reign of Julian the Apostate. That too was
a period of falling away from the Christian Church and
an espousing of the religion of paganism and philosophy.
The movement had the backing of the Emperor and every
advantage was given to those who would help revive the
old gods. But it was a lost cause and men proved unwilling
to give up Christianity for a dying polytheism.

So it has been with us. Barbarism has had its day and

too many men who should have known better, were attracted to it. Authority, blood and soil, ruthlessness, totalitarianism, fascism, nazism, communism, are some of the labels it bore. But under it all there was a revolt against Christianity and an attempt to set up a rival faith. That attempt, for the time being, has failed. When we saw where this thing led and what it did to its own followers, many a man saw Christianity in a new light. It was no longer a harmless proposition based on ancient legends and myths. John Baillie writes:

> I am happy to count among my own friends a rather remarkable number of men of high intellectual distinction who have returned to the full Christian outlook after years of defection from it, and I should say that in practically every case the renewed hospitality of their minds to Christian truth came about through their awakening to the essential untenability of the alternative positions which they had been previously attempting to occupy.[1]

We may go even further than this. A great number of thinking people are now convinced that ethics is no substitute for religion. They have learned that even a crude religion has more power than the most intelligent of ethical systems. We have seen hoodlums, with a fanatical faith so full of absurdities a high school sophomore could riddle it logically, march roughshod over the universities and the liberal thinkers. It may be only in a vague way, but the majority of people are in favor of Christianity. There is a new opportunity for the Christian cause to be heard in many circles that were closed to it twenty years ago.

An increasing intellectual vigor is apparent within the Christian faith. The most realistic thinking about the contemporary crisis is being done within the confines of the Christian Church. We have thinkers of rare ability putting the cause of theism on a firm foundation intellectually.

[1] Baillie, *Invitation to Pilgrimage*, Scribner's, 1926.

This of course is important. The Christian criticism of life has to be convincing to our intellectual leaders, and those who are serving the Church by making it so, put us forever in their debt.

But the distressing thing about the present situation is the number of men who have said yes to Christianity intellectually, and have stopped there. They talk vaguely about having their own religion and letting everybody else have his. They would no more think of associating themselves with their fellow Christians in a church, than they would think of standing on a street corner and confessing their sins. To attend the average church would be in the nature of a slumming expedition for many of them.

Now it needs to be pointed out that all who speak so blithely about the necessity of a spiritual revival but then keep aloof from the Church, are parasites. They have taken but they do not give. Where did they learn about the necessity of a spiritual revival? Where did their Christianity come from? Upon what foundation does Western civilization rest? To answer these questions honestly will show that they are very much in debt to this fellowship which they now despise.

There are certain weaknesses in the Church which none of us can deny. There are hypocrites in it. Men make pious commitments on Sunday and deny them on Monday. The most difficult people in the neighborhood to get along with are sometimes leaders in a church. Pious folk are too often the most stingy. But after belonging to many organizations and observing what their members agree to do and what they actually do, I come to the conclusion that there are at least a dozen other groups with more hypocrites per square inch than you will find in the Church per square yard. You will find more hypocrites at the symphony concert and at the opera. The man who stays apart from his brethren because some of them are pretenders, only reveals his own pride, and shows his need of fellowship. His halo is on too tight.

Much is made of our denominationalism and divisions. There is a point to this criticism. Yet much of the argument raised against the Church on this ground is about the same as some of Clarence Darrow's arguments against Christianity. He often set up straw men and knocked them down with a great flourish. He never seemed to realize that Christianity moves, though slowly, and that the Church is full of people who felt the same as he did about the Tennessee monkey trial.

It has been a long time since many of us have been aware of denominational strife and bitterness. We meet together and stand together in our witness to our communities. We are not willing to give up our traditions and heritages, and I do not see why we should. Religion is the most individual thing in the world, and it is not to be decried that men of different temperament look at it from different points of view. It is amazing how many people still assume that there is a bitter and bigoted fight going on between all the churches. This is simply untrue.

Men have their clubs and lodges. Women form groups of common interest. Yet they suddenly are outraged when Christians come together in congenial groups. The diversity of the Church is one of its glories, and I for one hope that we shall never have an organic union. There still are advances to be made in uniting for common enterprises, but to say that denominationalism is all bad is pure nonsense.

The minister is in danger of seeing the Church only from a professional angle. He finds himself out of sympathy with much modern criticism. To escape this as far as possible, I make it a point to be a member of a congregation whenever I am on my vacation. That is not enough, it is true, but over a period of the past years, I have come to certain unpalatable conclusions about Protestant church services.

For one thing, the music is often bad. That cannot always be helped. But even when there are competent musicians, too often they treat the congregation as if it were an audience at a concert. It is a professional show, which means that the self-consciousness of the artist is too apparent. Music in church ought to help men worship God and not merely be an artist's opportunity to show his talent. The great advantage of having the choir in the back of the sanctuary is that it helps to eliminate the concert atmosphere. Now and again one finds church music that seems to take the soul to God, and that is a great experience.

The preacher is often far from what he ought to be. No one can expect great preaching in every church and at every service. But one ought to expect careful preparation and hard work behind the sermon. Too many sermons are careless and show the touch of an undisciplined mind. There is a sort of casualness about them that is not fitting for the delivery of an urgent message.

Too often, the members of the congregation seem to lack any idea of why they are there. There is noise during every quiet moment in the service. There is rudeness on the part of individuals. There is coldness and aloofness. I am not one who appreciates a dozen people in the vestibule waiting to shake hands with me. All I want is a friendly greeting and a worshiping congregation. One expects that a church congregation will be different from any other kind of audience. Too often it is not.

With these and many other inadequacies, can any good come from the Church? It seems almost foolish to say that upon this institution there rests the hope of our world. But when we examine the alternatives, we are driven to believe that it is the Church or nothing. Historically, this much despised Church with its bickering and its human frailty has proved to be the rock upon which our defense against darkness and death has been built. God could in all probability produce His saints in a vacuum. But God does not do it that way. If the Church persecutes the prophets, the Church also produces them. No man has a right to speak about the spiritual needs of today unless he intends to do something more about it than speak. And if he decides he must act to restore faith to the world, he will be driven to the Church. For "the insufficiency of individual religion" is apparent of any thinking man.

Preservation

A few years ago I was asked to teach a college course on the relation between Christianity and Western civilization. The title finally chosen was "The Difference Christianity Has Made." It was a great experience to study our past and try to determine where our religion entered the picture and what results it had obtained. One of the things which still stands out in my mind is the number of times the Church has played the role of preserving some precious thing that would otherwise have been lost.

Probably the outstanding example is the part the Church played during the Dark Ages. There was not a great deal that could be done at that moment in the way of a constructive program. It was a time of waiting. But in those days, the Church preserved the heritage from Greece and Rome to be passed on when the fullness of time came. Or we may think of the Quakers and the slavery question. John Woolman did not find it possible to launch a full-fledged attack in the beginning. But within the Quaker fellowship there was preserved the sense of slavery's wrong until the attack against it could be made.

The Church often appears to be on its last legs. Carlyle said it was always that way. Its future seems precarious and many a time its imminent decease has been prophesied. But it is tougher than it looks. When it gets hold of a human value, it hangs on to it with tenacity. It is remarkable how little has been passed on to the future through groups of religious intelligentsia who have remained outside the Church. They are not big enough. They have too little of the truth. As Chesterton once said, every heresy is an attempt to narrow the Church. It has to be big enough to preserve many values.

There is always a need for conservation in society. The true conservative will not let go of that which if lost will make mankind the poorer. We become impatient with the Church because it does not move very fast. Sometimes it seems to us that it is hopelessly old fashioned and at least nineteen hundred years behind the times. In a sense, it is and in a sense it ought to be. A nation given over to fads would soon lose its way without groups of people not easily swayed by fads. The Church itself has its faddists, but there are always enough people who remember what happened in the past, to keep things steady.

Hours of crisis are always testing hours. They test our faith and our stability. They reveal the empty values which too many people have been assuming were dependable. In the crisis, we stand revealed for what we are, for there is never time either to patch things up or to put on a good appearance. It is then that we fall back on reservoirs built up in happier times. So it is with a society. In the hour of its crisis, it is dependent on what has been stored up. It is dependent on the stability and vigor of its institutions. It is at the mercy of its spiritual reserves. In the testing times, it becomes apparent that the Church is a preserver of society.

The modern home is not up to maintaining our spiritual heritage. One of the serious things is the number of parents who had a religious training themselves, but hope that somehow their children will get religion without any formal training. They look aghast at some of the results of this policy, but what did they expect? With the home on shaky foundations, the Church as a preserver of our spiritual heritage becomes even more important.

The school certainly has not been able to fulfill this function. As long as we hold to our secular emphasis in our educational philosophy, we may not expect that educated people will necessarily know anything about spiritual truth. In the very day when so many people have neglected the Church, it has become more vital to our society than ever before. Unless we find a substitute, we had better accept its claim on us.

The insufficiency of individual religion is nowhere more apparent than when we think of our relation to the past and to the future. Am I an isolated fact without roots or future? Do I owe anything to the past? Have I any obligation to the future? If I am a debtor to the past and will in turn be someone's ancestor, then I must make provision against time. I need to invest in something that will keep what I have committed unto it and pass it on to the next generation.

Among the rules laid down by a Chicago firm some eighty years ago, were the following: "Each employee must pay not less than $5.00 a year to the church and must attend Sunday school regularly. Men employees are given one evening a week for courting and two if they attend prayer meeting." The interesting point about this is the assumption that business has a stake in the institution of religion. One of the things we need to see again is that the great preservative force in any nation at any time is the Church. Because every man has a responsibility to his society, he owes it to the future to stand within its courts.

Prevention

The Church is a preventing institution. There are some things that do not happen if the Church is strong and alert. Society is full of waiting beasts of prey who dare not spring until the bars are down and the watchers have dozed. A spiritually dead people never see the danger until it is too late. But the Church has a long history of dealing with the enemies of the human spirit and long before most people can see what is happening, it gives its warning.

What would have happened in the times of persecution, if the world could have dealt only with individuals? At the end of the Roman Empire, how easily separate Christians could have been scattered and lost. One cannot escape the conclusion that without the Church, disintegrating forces would have had their way many a time. It is so often the rallying center for the defenders of decency. It is not easy to keep life decent, and it demands constant effort. Time after time when vulgarity or immorality began to march, it has been challenged and finally halted by the Church.

The word "Protestant" has too negative a sound for many ears. Some of our leaders have urged that we call ourselves "Evangelicals" and rid ourselves of a name which carries the wrong connotation. But a Protestant is one who bears witness. A good part of our task is to protest, and by our protesting, prevent. It is alarming to note how few people are willing to speak out against what may be a popular policy. Vaguely they may feel certain doubts about the advisability of what is proposed, but they are not enough concerned to say anything. The Church through its official pronouncements and its preaching witness, speaks out against tendencies which, if left unchallenged, would betray us.

Some years ago there was a little story written called *Angry Dust*. One man asked, "What is the devil?" Before anyone could reply, he answered his own question in these words: "The devil is not a huge monster with horns and a harpoon tail and a wicked glint in his eye. No, the devil is just taking the line of least resistance. It is inertia. It is doing nothing." At least this is that spirit which the devil counts as one of his chief allies. The Church protests when other groups are too busy or too fearful.

In our time, where does the protest come from, when seeds sown by the war begin to spring up? Where shall we turn to find support for the opposition against an increased military control of our life? If we escape this domination, we shall be under a great debt to the churches of America who have warned against the military becoming the master instead of the servant of the people. It has been Church leaders who have been alert to this danger.

Where do we look for protests against injustice to our minority groups? Certainly not to the patriotic organizations who shout the loudest about Americanism. It has been the Church that has dared to take its stand against a distorted interpretation of our democracy that makes it more in harmony with something out of *Mein Kampf*. It was a Protestant minister who challenged a rank instance of hate and injustice to a returned Japanese-American soldier on the West Coast.

A few years ago, I was thrilled at a Chinese Christian Student Conference held in Nevada. It was the time when the Japanese had been moved from the Coast inland, and it was the time when China was going through the brutal and savage invasion by the Japanese. But at the close of the Conference, a resolution was passed condemning the wholesale removal of the Japanese-Americans. "For," said those students, "when one minority's rights are overridden, every minority is in danger." Where else might one expect to hear such clear speech in a time of war?

There are times when whole peoples are swept with tidal waves of hate and lust. It is possible for an entire generation to be deluged with evil. Sometimes a nation has chosen to go with the current of materialism and expediency. Against such forces a people will do well to erect dams, for in such a time as we think not, these floods are upon us.

The Church does not always have a perfect record and it can become a part of the madness too. But there is more chance of its maintaining sanity, for it has been open to the sanity of Jesus' teaching. At least in recent times we have seen the Church stand as a dam against the flood tide of Hitler and his kind.

Anyone who has tried to get a politician to commit himself just before an election, knows how difficult it is. That is the time for silence and a benevolent neutrality. Ask a business leader to take a stand that may antagonize some of his customers and see how few there be who want to be counted. There are great exceptions to this general rule in every community. But a willingness to speak plainly in protest, is not a common characteristic. When it comes to this, the Church is the best hope. To its insistence on its right to speak, we owe more than we can ever tell. Said John Henry Newman: "Not a man in Europe who talks bravely against the Church but owes it to the Church he can talk at all." An institution with a record like that, deserves the support of every serious person.

Proclamation

Rebecca West said men forget truth that is too complicated and truth that is too simple. Perhaps we may just say frankly that men forget. They are in need of voices to tell them with regularity what is first and what is real. Judaism's protection in exile and persecution was her faith maintained through teaching:

> And these words, which I command thee this day, shall be upon thy heart; and thou shalt teach them diligently unto thy children, and shalt talk of them when thou sittest in thy house, and when thou walkest by the way, and when thou liest down, and when thou risest up. And thou shalt bind them for a sign upon thy hand, and they shall be for frontlets between thine eyes. And thou shalt write them upon the door-posts of thy house, and upon thy gates.
>   DEUTERONOMY 6:6-9

They were not so naïve as to think that faith is breathed in like air. It is taught and proclaimed.

Church attendance may not always be what it ought to be. But compared to any other kind of assembly, it is marvelous. Where else do people gather each week in numbers to compare with churchgoers? On what other subject could a man expect to speak year after year and have an audience? It is the old, old story, but it is still the story with the greatest appeal of all. The preacher soon learns that so long as he has the Bible and the Holy Spirit, he can preach forever and the message will be eagerly attended.

Silence the pulpits and you will take from the land the freest platform in the land. Nowhere else can a man have the freedom of speech which he enjoys in a Protestant pulpit. So the Church provides a place where the Gospel can be proclaimed for me and to me. I need to be reminded. I need to take some responsibility in reminding others. For both of these personal needs, the Church gives the answer.

When a man who has formed the good habit of regular church attendance stays home on a Sunday to join his friends in some secular enterprise, he will feel differently the whole week. It is not easy to explain why, nor does he know just what he missed most. But he knows that to be with his Christian brethren in worship, reminds him of things he can so easily forget, and tells him about a world which is easily crowded from his thinking by the affairs of the market place.

In the early days, the radio was looked upon by some as a rival to the Church. We were told that a few great voices would send the message to the homes of the multitude. Sometimes a church hesitated to broadcast its service for fear that it would lessen attendance. The fears were unjustified. You can listen to a lecture or a forum over the air and miss very little. But a sermon is part of a larger experience which cannot come over the airwaves. People need the whole atmosphere of the Church to proclaim what they so easily forget but what no life can afford to forget.

A young man stood beside the sickbed of his aged father. The old man's hands were knotted, his face was rough, for he had lived a hard life. His language was not that of the educated man. But as the boy thought of it later, he said, "I looked upon that rough face and I realized that many of the burdens which he had carried, and the pains he had suffered, had been that I might have my chance. Suddenly, and for the first time, my father appeared beautiful." And when we think of what the Church has done for us through the years, we say:

> How beautiful upon the mountains are the feet of him that bringeth good tidings, that publisheth peace, that bringeth good tidings of good, that publisheth salvation, that saith unto Zion, Thy God reigneth!   ISAIAH 52:7

Production

Men need to be saved from "the angelic fallacy." We are not angels but men, and men must work to produce a better world. It will not come automatically but as the result of the united efforts of men bound together in a fellowship. This is what the Church provides. Jesus did not organize the Church but he did something more—he created it. It was inevitable that men who had been with him could not be satisfied to let his creative influence fade. The Church became his body to carry on his activities.

When one begins to trace the origins of the best products of our civilization, it is discovered that most of them come either directly or indirectly from the Church. What we often assume just happened, proves upon investigation to have the efforts and the sacrifices of the Christian fellowship behind it. For any man who thinks the Church is merely decorative, a study of where we got our education, our concern for the sick and the poor, our respect for women, our feeling of obligation for children, and a host of other marks of the civilized man, will convince him that the Church has produced fruits.

The record of the Christian Church during the war has been a glorious one. It did not split apart into nationalistic parts. It won the admiration of former critics by its heroism in the lands under the heel of tyranny. It kept us steady when we were being bombarded with the propaganda of hatred. It kept its head under the most difficult of circumstances.

But the great product of the Church today is the World Fellowship of Christians. As the late archbishop of Canterbury said, it is the great new fact of our time. We know now that a blueprint will never produce one world. It demands a world public opinion. The one institution producing that opinion is the Church. No man can belong to it without getting a world vision and developing a world mind. The young men who were sent to the far places during the war, were often surprised and tremendously impressed when they learned the Church was there first.

The Church is playing the part of a guinea pig in this business of building a world community. We are facing the difficulties and the obstacles that must be faced when men endeavor to cut across their differences. There come to my desk from time to time, bulletins from the World Council of Churches in Geneva. When men say to us that it is impossible to create unity among men of different races and nations, we can say to them that we know it is possible because we are doing it. This is no longer in the theory stage. It has become a reality. No other organization is so widely spread as the Christian Church. Let no minister nor layman forget that he belongs to a world-wide fellowship in a world that seems bent on splitting apart. One of the things that amazes me most is the way men can spend their time in joining a hundred and one organizations but keep aloof from the one that means more than all the rest put together.

When Hell Gate Bridge was being constructed to link New England with the South, a caisson had to be sunk in a certain spot in the East River. But on this spot they found a sunken barge which was immovable. Five tugs could not lift that half-buried barge. Then a workman suggested they use the tide. So at low tide, a flat boat was fastened to the barge with cables. When the tide came in with its irresistible power, the barge was lifted and the pier could be built. Which is a parable! The obstacles in the way of our building bridges across the chasms which separate us, can only be removed by the mighty power of God. But He must have something with which He can work, and that something is the World Fellowship of Christians. What man among us dare say that he is excused from being a part of that lifting instrument? The Church has helped to create and maintain the Christian mind. It deserves our love and our devotion.

X

HERITAGE AND DESTINY

". . . the Father, from whom every family in heaven and on earth is named . . ."

EPHESIANS 3:14

People with social background and standing always seem so self-confident that many of us can hardly keep envy from our hearts. Youngsters learn that the lines are drawn very early. There is an indescribable something which unites some groups and keeps others out. It is not a matter of intelligence, nor even of wealth. It is just that some belong and some do not.

The Chinese are not the only ones who are ancestor worshipers. One of our governors, when asked by John Gunther what he believed in most, answered, "My family." Attend any historical society meeting and you come away with the feeling of having been immersed in a sort of genealogical fatalism. Woe unto the man who is not a native son or the son of a pioneer. All of this has the power of appealing to snobbery and not many of us are entirely free of it. If we do not really belong to the "best families" we wish that we did, and we make the best of what we have.

Now part of this desire for a good background is entirely legitimate. We live in a lonely place and our life is a transitory thing. The drifting rootlessness of much modern living leaves us unsatisfied and just a little frightened. Plato said that a man is like a tree walking upside down—his roots are in the air. But wherever his roots are, a man needs to feel that they are fixed in some nourishing soil. The past has an appeal because we want to believe we belong to something that began before our arrival here. The genealogist feeds that need. There is no denying that a long and honorable family history gives a man more assurance and stability than comes to the drifter. But this need is so often treated too cheaply. A great past will not compensate for a trivial present. My father's achievements are mine only by right of deserving them. The attempt to pay honor at the graves of our ancestors while we deny their spirit, will not compensate us for our loss of worth.

Some years ago, a book was published entitled *Give Yourself a Background,* and it became a best seller. It was a sort of "how to win friends" discussion and gave the things a man ought to know in order to impress people with his intellectual standing. The general idea was that anyone could pick up enough facts to sprinkle through his conversation so that his listeners would be much impressed with the breadth of his knowledge and experience. This kind of thing falls into the general category of learning to speak French in order to impress the waiter, or learning to play the piano in ten easy lessons so as to become the life of the party.

The thing which this kind of philosophy cannot seem to grasp is that surface tricks are apparent to anyone with half a brain. The most boring person in the world is the one whose accomplishments are all for effect. Try going about showing off your background by telling people how much you know about this and that, if you want to be the most unpopular person in the group. Background is something you either have or have not, and the person who truly has it is usually unconscious of it. This assurance is a thing of the heart.

Yet a background is more a matter of achievement than it is of inheritance. Men learn to feel at home in this universe because of what they are. This does not necessarily have anything to do with our pedigree. It is a matter of finding reality and adjusting ourselves to it. It is striking that narrow balance between a respect for the past and a refusal to be enslaved by it. It is a matter of being respectful of the past but uncaptured by it. For a background ought to provide not only serenity but inspiration.

Whenever I begin to think about this, there comes the picture of St. Paul writing to the Corinthians. He says to them:

> Wherefore let no one glory in men. For all things are yours; whether Paul, or Apollos, or Cephas, or the world, or life, or death, or things present, or things to come; all are yours; and ye are Christ's; and Christ is God's.
> I CORINTHIANS 3:21-23

How could he speak such words to those people? If ever a group seemed doomed to be on the outside of things, it was the early Christians. But Paul wanted them to feel they belonged to the future and were the heirs of the ages. For if they belonged to Christ, then they belonged to God. They were the chosen people. They had a background that provided them with an unlimited future.

It is this experience that so many Christians miss. They have heard a few notes of the orchestra, but have not heard the complete symphony. They are aware of their own denomination and their local church. They do not know from whence they have come and what they are destined to become. They have never felt their hearts lifted as they contemplated the saints and martyrs whose spiritual children they are. Desperately they seek some significance for their living, in groups centered about secondary ideals. But these people need to have their eyes opened to that mighty fellowship of Christ.

I have an old friend who stops by now and again to talk for a few moments about his Christian experiences. No one could claim that he is the most gifted man in the world. He has very little education, and when it comes to worldly wisdom, he is almost naïve. But the one thing that impresses me most about him, is his quiet assumption that he belongs to a fellowship that is like a great family. Often he will say, in discussing something that seems mysterious: "I do not know the answer to that, but my Elder Brother knows." In this fine old Christian's heart there is never a trace of envy for those who may possess a social standing far above him. He has a background. The Christian belongs to the greatest family in the world, for his brother is Christ, and his father is God.

Our Father

We begin with God here as we must in all the serious quests of life. To be at home, we must find our Father's house and get in harmony with our Father's will. The world is ever a madhouse to the man estranged from God.

It has no meaning until we are under His orders. Omar Khayyám describes this lost feeling:

> Yesterday This Day's Madness did prepare;
> Tomorrow's Silence, Triumph, or Despair;
> Drink! for you know not whence you came, nor why:
> Drink! for you know not why you go nor where.[1]

No man apart from God can long feel at home here. The more we talk about "Mother Earth," the more we reveal our loneliness and longing. The earth is not our mother and this is not our resting place. To the man who tries to make the grave the end of his journey, there is never anything but anguish and homesickness. The hedonist tries to ease the feeling by seeking pleasure. But the body after a while becomes satiated and the ache is still there. Lucretius preached that immortality is a false doctrine and should be repudiated. He tried to rob death of any fear by pointing out that at its worst, it was only the cessation of life. But it is all in vain. Earth is not enough.

The humanists who would make this world the limit of the human adventure, are not able to convince us. We listen and may try to believe it for a time, but this doctrine does not bring us contentment and there is no peace in contemplating it. It is a rather pitiful cry of defeat when one of them says to his fellows, "You see, all we have is each other."

Heaven is our destination and earth is not and cannot be our final home. This is the word of God to Abraham:

> Know of a surety that thy seed shall be a stranger in a
> land that is not theirs . . .   GENESIS 15:13

Remember the cry of the Psalmist:

> How shall we sing the Lord's song in a strange land?
>   PSALM 137:4

[1] Fitzgerald, *The Rubáiyát of Omar Khayyám.*

This universal human experience has sometimes been interpreted as being the reason for religion. Freud and his school thought it proved that religion is an illusion. But it can also be an indication that men are not content here because they are made for another world. It may mean that God has placed this homesickness in us so that we will seek Him. At least the heart of the Christian experience is that when men are found by God, they feel they belong, and their homesickness for a future is taken away.

The insistence of our religion that we must always put God first, is one of its hardest sayings. So many other things clamor for our attention. We have the feeling that matters nearer at hand ought to come first. God can wait. But when Jesus gives us the model prayer, it begins with "Our Father." In all of his teaching there is the assumption that nothing will go right with us until we find God.

The human impulse is to center our attention on ourselves. We seek a background that will enlarge our egos. We want an answer that will heighten our self-centeredness. Here is the eternal conflict between human perversity and God. He seeks to make us expand and we try to close in upon ourselves and build higher barriers to protect us. He seeks to help us forget ourselves, and we want to forget everything else but ourselves. We begin with our own little world, and we close our eyes to everything beyond, marking it as unknown and, therefore, dangerous territory.

With this fearfulness as a beginning, everything we do only increases our desperation. Too much prayer simply accentuates what is already wrong with us. Instead of being freed from our selfishness, our prayer only increases it. Aldous Huxley spoke of the "God's-eye view." Until we can ask to be given that and without further reservation center our minds on Him, our praying is only vain repetition and an animal cry for help.

The truth is that there is no horror quite as bad as seeing

nothing beyond ourselves. Yet so perverse is our nature that we will not let Him show us the far views of His plans for His children. We build a little hall of mirrors until the constant looking at ourselves makes us dizzy with hopelessness. The contradictions within us are unsolvable by our efforts. We are under a law of sin and death until we put ourselves under His law of love. St. Paul says it in these words:

> But we all, with unveiled face beholding as in a mirror the glory of the Lord, are transformed into the same image from glory to glory, even as from the Lord the Spirit.
> II CORINTHIANS 3:18

What can be done about human perversity? The only thing to be done is confess to God that we can do nothing. We come to Him with these warring elements within us and we tell Him quite simply that they are beyond us. We want God to come to us, but we run from His presence. It would seem that even God cannot help such crazy creatures as we are. So we must come bringing our contradictions with us—our desire for purity and our love for uncleanness, our hunger for truth and our willingness to lie, our desire for courage and our lust for ease. Then He comes to heal our moral anarchy with a miracle of saving grace. Then we are at home and our pilgrimage becomes a triumphant march.

The Moral Law

The physical universe never became a place worthy of our trust until the laws governing it began to be revealed. As long as men lived in the midst of unpredictable happenings, they never knew what to expect. The earth was full of terror by night and uncertainty by day. What a great thing science has accomplished in revealing an orderly universe. Man may seem small and inconsequential in the light of the solar system, but he is a giant when one thinks of his knowl-edge of that system. Yet strangely enough, this knowledge which ought to make us more at home, has dwarfed the feeling of significance for many men so that they are more fearful now than ever before. It is often a case of egotism on a cosmic scale. If the universe is so large and the earth is no longer the center, we are afraid of our destiny.

We need to understand the moral law. This invisible machinery of life proclaims the spiritual nature of God. When once it dawns on us that the same power which made the stars also ordained the final triumph of goodness and the ultimate overthrow of evil, we begin to see that there is vastly more here than just physical power. Many a man who complains because life will not give him what he wants, is like a fretting infant who is not mature enough to understand a parent's love. The great thing about the moral law is that when we are willing to sit before it and learn, the world loses its vast emptiness. What formerly seemed to be a stubborn obstacle in our way, becomes the sign of a Presence in whose love we are safe.

Whenever we try to brutally assert our wills on life and wring from it obedience to our desires, we are heading for disaster. For the time being we may feel that we have cured our loneliness. But it is the false promise of pride which whispers to us: "You are God." We think the answer to our fear is bluster and it seems that the whisper of the still small voice can be silenced by our loud shouting.

The greatest mistake we can make is to attempt the over-coming of our inferiority by asserting superiority over others. A nation following that path will find it is not moving toward a safe place for itself, but only postponing its own destruction. Let America face that now. This is not to be the American Century or the Russian Century. This like every century belongs to the moral law. It is never abrogated and it will not be adjusted to suit us or anyone else. The moral law is universal and has no favorites. It was because Jesus saw this so clearly that he spoke the words of the Beatitudes. They are a picture of life lived against the background of God and the description of the quiet confidence of sons of God. They are, in a word, a portrait of men who live on a level beyond the reach of the boasting, frightened, power-mad cowards.

One might imagine a happening like this at the time of the Crucifixion. A man is at his bench when the procession goes by on its way to Calvary. He goes to the doorway and stands there as the soldiers pass with their three prisoners. "Who are they?" he asks one of his fellows. "Just two thieves and that strange prophet from Galilee," is the answer. "Well," says the workman as he turns back to his bench, "he didn't last long, did he? They got rid of him in a hurry." Yet nineteen centuries later that one they got rid of is the reality against which the empires are broken. His whole career is a sign of moral reality which is indestructible. We live in a moral world, and Christians are at home in it.

Sympathy

Will Rogers said he never knew a man he didn't like. Most of our animosities are born from ignorance and suspicion. Seldom does one get acquainted with another man that he does not feel he has found a brother. We may not be as fond of some people as others, but men always have more in common than they have to keep them apart. Sympathy with others is something we can learn. Men often act on the supposition that if they meet a stranger, they should throw a brick at him. But men can learn to meet strangers with an honest attempt to find reasons for appreciation.

Turgenev and Tolstoy were walking together down a country lane when they saw an old broken-down horse standing alone in a field. Tolstoy crawled through the fence and went over to the horse. Putting his hand on the animal's neck he began to talk to him. Turgenev said he talked with such sympathy and understanding that he thought Tolstoy must have at one time been a horse. That is one of the reasons why he could be a great writer. He had learned sympathy for every living creature. The men who have learned their kinship with all of life, begin to lose their fear of life.

Those who come to feel that every man's hand is against them and that the only way to survive is to strike first, need to deliberately seek other points of view from their own. There is a line in the story of Jesus crossing the sea of Galilee which might be interpreted as describing his attitude of sympathy. Mark relates that Jesus said to his disciples, "Let us go over unto the other side" (Mark 4:35). He was always doing that himself and helping men to cross over in their thinking and their sympathy.

How different things look from the other side! We learn that men are not always bad and antagonistic. They are simply looking at things from a different point. The American Revolution hardly seems to be the same event when it is read in an English history book and then compared with the orthodox American version. It is not true that one side is right and the other wrong. Probably they are both right and they are both wrong. But it helps us to see that the world is made up of people who have to look at things from where they are and, of course, from the viewpoint of what they are.

Today we are being driven to the position of facing an inevitable enemy. One of my friends said to me, "I'd give anything in the world if I could understand what the ordinary man in Russia is thinking." The little knowledge that has come to us from behind the Iron Curtain, suggests that the ordinary man in Russia is thinking very much the same as the ordinary man in any country. Reports of most foreign correspondents indicate that there is as much fear of

war in their hearts as there is in mine. Once we can be convinced that another person or another nation is deliberately
evil, as opposed to our goodness, we are afraid. If we can
believe that all of us are blunderers and all of us are sinners, but that fundamentally we want about the same things,
we can begin to feel at home in the world with all our
differences.

What do you think the history of Africa would be if it
were written by the natives of Africa? Would it be a glorious story of conquest and the discovery of riches? No, it
would be a sordid story of enslavement, cruelty, and thiev-
ery. Which is the true story of Africa? Certainly we cannot
expect the true story from our side alone. We must cross
over, and associate ourselves with the poor and the disin-
herited. On what basis have we any right to assert that our
interpretations must be right?

I am impressed with the number of novelists who are
trying to interpret our persecuted minorities to us, and that
is good. One man tells what happened to Negro troops
stationed in England. Another writes about a white man
who finds he has Negro blood and takes his place with the
Negro race. Still another tells about a man who becomes a
Jew in order to write about anti-Semitism. These books are
written on the supposition that the hatreds will go and the
fears will be lifted when we learn to have sympathy. We
must learn to enter into relationships with all men so that
what they suffer, we suffer. When our hearts become hard-
ened, then we shut ourselves off from being confident and
unafraid.

When Ezekiel joined his people in their exile, he said:

> Then I came to them of the captivity at Tel-abib, that
> dwelt by the river of Chebar, and I sat where they sat . . .
>   EZEKIEL 3:15

This is what the Christian is to do. His background is as

wide as the world. He belongs not to a favored class or nation, but to men who are the sons of one Father.

Brotherhood

Once we can believe that all men are brothers, we can have the sense of being a part of a great family. All the best in the family belongs to me and I have a right to claim any member of it. I am a part of all mankind, and I belong with all those whom I understand and love.

Now the foundation of any belief we may have, is the reason we hold for its being true. The wrong reasons may support the belief for a time, but they never can make it secure. It is terribly important that our faith should rest on the right reasons. There are a great number of well-meaning people who are striving to believe in brotherhood these days, but their reasons are wrong. They may argue that we should love the Chinese because he is just as bright as we are. The anthropological arguments happen to support that belief. Or it may be argued that brotherhood is to be practiced because the other race, wherever it has had a chance, has proved as adaptable to civilization as our own. You may say that human blood is all the same and it happens science says that is true, the Red Cross policy notwithstanding. But none of these reasons are right for the Christian.

In the memoranda of Abraham Lincoln written about the time of the debates with Stephen Douglas, there is the following note:

> If A can prove, however conclusively, that he may, of right, enslave B, why may not B snatch the same argument, and prove equally that he may enslave A? You say A is white and B is black. It is color, then: the lighter, having the right to enslave the darker? Take care. By this rule, you are to be slave to the first man you meet with a fairer skin than your own. You do not mean color exactly? You mean the whites are intellectually the superiors of the blacks, and therefore,

have the right to enslave them? Take care again. By this rule, you are to be slave to the first man you meet, with an intellect superior to your own. But, say you, it is a question of interest: and if you can make it to your interest, you have the right to enslave another? Very well, And if he can make it his interest, he has the right to enslave you.

What Lincoln saw so clearly as he thought through this problem, was that the wrong reason for believing in slavery will lead a man into contradictions. And so will the wrong reason for believing in brotherhood.

It happens that science is on the side of brotherhood. It happens that the anthropologists are on that side. But if they were not, that would make no difference to the Christian belief. For men are brothers regardless of equality or ability. They are brothers even if one race has to carry the larger share of the burden. They are brothers because God made them, and Christ died for them.

This business of brotherhood often is put on too sentimental a basis. Men feel a momentary pity, shed a few tears, and then wall themselves into their former tight race consciousness. Richard Wright, the Negro writer, wrote some stories called *Uncle Tom's Children*. Later he said:

> I realized that I had made an awfully naïve mistake. I found I had written a book which even bankers' daughters could read and weep over and feel good about. I swore to myself that if I ever wrote another book, no one would weep over it; that it would be so hard and deep that they would have to face it without the consolation of tears.

Brotherhood is something to accept because it is realism and not because it is romantic. It is the way things are and its denial is like breaking up a home.

This is the way Paul put it in his speech to the Athenians:

> The God that made the world and all things therein, he, being Lord of heaven and earth, dwelleth not in temples made with hands; neither is he served by men's hands, as

> though he needed anything, seeing he himself giveth to all
> life, and breath, and all things; and he made of one every
> nation of men to dwell on all the face of the earth, having
> determined their appointed seasons, and the bounds of
> their habitation . . . ACTS 17:24-26

This is an affirmation of faith that follows naturally and
inevitably from his understanding of God.

Racial pride and racial hatred are not things to be removed by argument. It is thought by some that if men can
be taught true ideas about their fellows, they will lose
their hatred. Prejudice, we are told, is ignorance. Does this
mean that when the Germans persecuted the Jews, it was
only because they were ignorant of the kind of people the
Jews were? Obviously not, for many of them had lived with
Jewish people for many years. Can we eliminate all race
riots and pogroms by education? I think not. Education will
help and should be encouraged, but it is only a partial
answer. For this bitter poison has its center in human pride.
We persecute because we want to assure ourselves that we
are superior to others. Hatred must be washed out of the
souls of men by God's love shed abroad in their hearts. It
is perfect love that casteth ·out fear. It is Jesus Christ who
teaches us how to love one another.

When Muretus, the Protestant scholar, fell ill in a strange
city, he was sent to a paupers' hospital. He overheard two
doctors talking in Latin. Said one of them, "Let us try an
experiment on this worthless fellow." And Muretus mur-
mured in Latin, "Will you call worthless, one for whom
Christ died?" This is the reason no man is worthless. This is
the reason we are bound together without regard to color
or station.

All men live in their Father's world, and it is under the
rule of His moral law. We are made with common aims and
needs. We are brethren for whom Christ died. We belong
to His family. We have a great past and we look forward to

a glorious future. We seem to be made for one another, all over the world. The Christian envies no man, for he has the greatest heritage and destiny of all. The Christian mind reaches up to God and across the wide boundaries of all mankind.

XI

THE REAL KINGDOM

> "... and of his kingdom there shall be no end."
>
> LUKE 1:33

The seriousness of our contemporary situation is not due primarily to the difficulties facing us. Too many people seem to assume that if the atom bomb had never been discovered, we would be all right. Or we assume that if only this or that potential enemy was curbed, we would find the world a pleasant place. But the truth is that none of these things is the real problem. The real problem is our lack of faith.

We begin to suspicion that we are not going to be saved by vitamins, or the right mouth wash. It will take more than General Motors. The tricks of salesmanship lose their power to arouse us. Gradually it begins to dawn upon us that there is still an empty place in our lives which none of the gadgets we have made can fill. Then comes the ultimate despair— there is no salvation. We are the victims of desperate men who have given final loyalty to relative values and persuaded their followers they could lead them on the road to heaven. As these visions have, one after another, turned into nightmares, we have grown less and less able to try again with any confidence. Let us look at some of these adventures in disillusionment.

First of all, consider the kingdom of our secularized democracy. This is an adventure that has lost its self-confidence. The history of America has been a paradox in that the stronger we have become, the more uncertain we are of the democratic way. That which began as a positive faith, has become more and more a huge machine with no spiritual center. What nourished our fathers in their hazardous adventure, does not feed their sons. We still use the words and the phrases, but they no longer have their old meanings. As a matter of fact, when a man uses the term "democracy" today, we are at once suspicious of what he has in mind. From what special vantage point is he looking? What special interest is he seeking to promote?

If we care to reminisce a bit, we might look back to the period between the two World Wars. In those days the self-confessed intelligentsia had a growing sense of democracy as something cheap, crude, vulgar, and materialistic. They developed a nostalgia for the Old World, and though most of them had never been there, they created a romantic picture of its life. They believed that it provided leisure, for a certain class at least, and provided the opportunity for the development of a real culture. But the main point was not that they were looking backward with wistful eyes, but that they were no longer looking forward down the democratic vistas with expectation.

Our democracy seemed to have developed a sordid selfishness that left us unenthusiastic. The boasting of our greatness, usually associated with Fourth of July orations, was only an object of ridicule. We began to feel that, as Pliny had said about Rome, America being unable to make its institutions beautiful, decided to make them big. There was a city which printed a folder in the year 1918 boasting that the population of the city would be 250,000 by 1930.

This seemed to be typical of the prevailing attitude. No one bothered to ask, "Two hundred and fifty thousand what?" We had become worshipers of quantity as an end in itself.

Self-interest became more prominent and the idealism of democracy faded into the background. Originally, we had thought that democracy was to liberate the common man and give him his chance for a fuller development. Although often denied in practice, we liked to remind ourselves of the welcome to all those who were oppressed in other lands, inscribed on the Statue of Liberty. But that idea, too, has faded. A commentator reported that many lawmakers were relieved when the President and legislative leaders agreed that in order for Congress to adjourn in July, 1947, there would be no time to consider admitting 400,000 displaced persons. Back of that simple statement there is the tragedy of a dead faith. There was a time when the spirit of democracy would have insisted this was such an important issue, that nothing must let it be crowded out of consideration. America seems to be willing to regard many things as more important than displaced persons, or indeed, than persons of any kind.

Professor Perry in *Puritanism and Democracy* tells about a dog he had when he was a boy. It chased cats, but if the cat refused to run and turned, the dog suddenly discovered he had an errand somewhere else, or he must stop and scratch a flea. Cats were to be chased, but not to be caught, and if the cat insisted on being caught, the dog was embarrassed. So Professor Perry says, the closer we have come to democracy, the less sure we are about it. We do not seem to know what to do with it. The war provided us with something of an awakening to the meaning of our democratic way, but it was not a rebirth of faith. It was only a shot in the arm and it is already wearing off.

One of the strangest and most serious things that has happened to us is the bringing home of the gods of our enemies.

We fought against militarism and racial hatred. We despised the high-handed methods of power-mad minorities in control of the people. But the emptiness of our democratic faith is nowhere more apparent than in the speed and ease with which these things have rushed into our vacuum. We are a living example of Jesus' parable of the seven devils rushing into the empty room. Democracy has been secularized and in the process, it has lost its confidence.

Fascism may be described as a kingdom that lost the war. But it had a considerable appeal before that happened, and it is far from dead. There came a time when the emptiness of human life made it necessary to turn from hollow phrases to something more positive, even if it were nothing more than a revolt against those spiritual affirmations we no longer believed. Instead of the equality of men, the vision of the superman, the pure race myth, and the worship of power caught the imagination of great numbers of men. We must not forget how close that idea came to winning a military victory. But it did not win, and by its own standards, that should be conclusive. It agreed to be tested on the basis of its accomplishments. Might makes right, it insisted, and if it was not mighty enough to win, then it has been judged by its own criterion. The spread of the fascist madness is another indication of the emptiness of what has often been called the Great Tradition. That Tradition was based on the Christian Faith and the humanistic spirit of the Enlightenment. It was the heritage of Western civilization.

The whole idea of elections and the ability of common men to govern themselves, was attacked by Hitler in that strange conglomeration of shrewdness and madness called *Mein Kampf*. The early inhabitants of Tombstone, Arizona, elected the most notorious desperado as sheriff in the hope that he would kill off some of his rivals and keep the rest of the outlaws under control. In the meantime, plain citizens would be allowed to mine in peace. It was a policy of desperation, even as the acceptance of fascism was a desperate confession of failure. In neither case did it work. The prisoners in the dock at the Nürnberg Trials were the symbols of the citizens of this kingdom. Only those who either hope to have a brilliant short period of personal glory, or those who are incapable of learning anything from experience, can equate the good life for mankind with fascism.

There is communism which is a kingdom without realism. During the war, we developed a sudden respect for the Soviets when they held the German horde back. Our red witch hunt was called off for the time being. We began to say that after all, they had something. We had greeted every substitute for democracy with that same word—"they have something." Now we are no longer allies, but rivals, and the witch hunt is on again with increased ferocity. We are willing for people to talk about Russia if they show things are bad there and we are as white-robed angels in comparison. It is difficult for us to get a fair appraisal of this rival.

My main impression of communism is its sentimentality. It believes that the troubles of the world have been due to the wrong people being in power, and if the dictatorship of the proletariat is established, all will be well. But it never asks a perfectly obvious question, namely, what is to prevent the same power from corrupting the proletariat that has already corrupted the capitalists? All of us are sinners, and I would not vote for preachers to rule their brethren any more than I would vote for any single group. Are things usually much better after revolutionists have taken the place of reactionaries? It is not apparent.

Communism provides for no self-criticism. It takes itself so seriously that it loses its willingness to be judged and discussed. On one thing all the erring brethren who finally leave the communist fold agree—it is an intellectual straitjacket. It seems to mesmerize its victims so that its converts lose their dignity and become crawling yes men for whatever the party line may be at the moment.

Why is communism so feared by democracy? Here we come to something very significant. It is feared because it is a secularism that still believes in itself, while our democracy is a secularism that no longer believes in itself. It is a threat to a materialistic democracy because it still has faith and we no longer believe in the adequacy of materialistic goals. We have been over that road, and we found it a dead end. But the communists still believe that for them it will lead to the promised land. We are like adults watching adolescents go through the same mistakes we made, only they are young and robust, while we are old and weary. We are afraid, and our fear is driving us on the road to reaction. To halt an expanding communism, we have nothing but dollars and guns.

We are men without a faith. In some ways, Stefan Zweig symbolizes our condition. On February 23, 1942, he committed suicide in Brazil. He was at the top of his profession as a writer. He was established comfortably in the South American country where he had gone after escaping from the Nazis. He had many friends. In the note left behind to explain his act, he said:

> Nowhere else would I have preferred to build up a new existence, the world of my own language having disappeared for me and my spiritual home, Europe, having destroyed itself. But after one's sixtieth year, unusual powers are needed in order to make another wholly new beginning. Those that I possess have been exhausted by long years of homeless wandering.

So we stand contemplating the future. The years of wandering are behind us and still we have not arrived. Where is the real kingdom? To what homeland may we turn? Where can our spirits be at peace? To these and kindred questions, we have an answer: The Kingdom of God.

The Kingdom of God is not something we must build. It has been one of our greatest blunders to assume that men must create it by sheer human persistence. The end result of that kind of effort is weariness and failure. We become tired liberals who see the building fall down as fast as we build it up. We conclude finally that we are the victims of a mirage. We seem to see a structure rising, but it is only a hallucination.

The Kingdom of God is. It is the essential nature of things. Our task is to understand that and to adjust our lives to it. Only to the extent that our human kingdoms partake of its nature, can they stand or satisfy us. It is a divine kingdom and cannot be taken by stealth or violence. It is taken by faith. It is inhabited by believers, and it is home to our hearts.

Citizenship

The great heresy of our time is the belief that getting can be substituted for being. Our worship of the cult of sensations is a sign of this heresy. It is not important to understand things, we believe, it is only important to know how to use them. Our heroes are manipulators and not philosophers. If we could only get enough stuff together, we have believed that we could very well do without character. No people have been under such a constant bombardment of endless invention, as we of this generation. Inventions can be used by anyone clever enough to push the buttons. That a man who pushed the button needed to be either a good man or a wise man, has not seemed to us reasonable.

This is the reason why our science has so outrun our morals. We have not believed that morals were any longer essential. This is the reason for our swing away from democracy as a guarantee of the dignity and rights of each man's life, to democracy as only a political system of representative government. We thought we were beyond the need for paying much heed to the inner qualities of life.

The Greek mythology was wise enough to point out that power and cleverness were not adequate substitutes for wisdom in personal relations. Remember Vulcan the god of conflagrations who could do such marvelous things with fire. But he was miserable and ridiculous because he could not keep his wife interested. Or in more recent times consider the psychological knowledge developed by the Germans. But of what value was it for them to study Freud and Adler and Münsterberg if all they succeeded in doing was to make themselves hated?

This is the age of the questionnaire and the survey. Too often such things are but a substitute for action. They act as a sort of emotional anodyne. Sometimes we spend much energy and money in the collecting of facts about our churches and their locations. But when it is all over, we still lack the power and the will to change the local situation very much. We become like the Mississippian who confessed, "I been 'ponderin' so hard I ain't had time to think."

Our trouble is summed up in a story about a country girl who married a city boy. She wrote home after a while that she had more nice clothes than ever before; she was meeting the kind of people she had always wanted to meet; she was traveling and she had always wanted to travel; she was going to all the theaters she could find time to attend. Then she added, "There is only one thing wrong. I hate my husband." We too can list all the things we have which our fathers did not have and we thought we wanted. But where there ought to be affection, there is hatred, and where there ought to be expectancy, there is a dull boredom. We have things, but we are not the kind of people who can enjoy them.

In this condition we hear the word of our Lord. He warns us of the mistake we make if we get things and lose our souls. He speaks of qualities of the inner life as if they were supreme. He tries to make us understand that love and simplicity are better than hate and riches. He brings us back to the unescapable truth of human experience that unless our personal relations are right, nothing is right. He points out to us that if we center our hearts on transitory values, they will leave our hearts barren. The important thing, says he, is to be something. For as long as the moral law operates we will get what we deserve. The only way to improve our life is to improve our deserving.

Is this not the gift of Christ to each man who comes to him? He takes our attention from quantity to quality. He directs our love away from the temporal to the eternal. He makes us new creatures because he releases us from our bondage to things. The Christian becomes a citizen of a new country. In the fine phrase of Ephesians:

> So then ye are no more strangers and sojourners, but ye are fellow-citizens with the saints, and of the household of God, being built upon the foundation of the apostles and prophets, Christ Jesus himself being the chief corner stone.
>
> EPHESIANS 2:19-20

Ansari of Herat said, "Can you walk on the water? So can a straw. Can you fly in the air? So can a bluebottle. Conquer your heart, and then you will be somebody." There is no real improvement anywhere but in the heart. No kingdom can do anything for its citizens if it cannot encourage progress within. The end result of any way of life, is the kind of people it produces. The Kingdom of God is the real kingdom for it is only under His rule that our lives can become better.

When J. W. Dunne came to the conclusion that in his dreams he was seeing not only the past but sometimes the future, he drew up that interesting philosophy called "Serialism." It regards time not as a flowing stream between rigid banks but as another dimension. Christians know that in Christ they experience eternity breaking into their transitory lives. It is a new dimension that redeems men caught in the monotony of a flatland of things. It restores being to the center of our living and saves us from the boredom of getting.

Service

One of the greatest temptations we have to face is the tendency to insulate ourselves from men. We move in a certain circle and we develop a certain group of friends. Before we know what has happened to us, we have come to think of that group as more important than all the rest of mankind together. We become class people, thinking class thoughts, limited to class sympathies. Against any threat to our group standards or privileges, we set our faces with hatred. Life becomes for too many people a narrowing process.

During the war when there was gasoline rationing, a wealthy lady found it necessary to ride to the opera on the subway. The car was crowded, and as she clung to a strap with her nose lifted disdainfully, she said to her escort, "I haven't ridden in one of these smelly subways in years." An old man seated a few seats away looked up from his paper and said, "Lady, we've missed you." Too many people with superior talents and abilities have been missed from sharing the common burdens of men.

In the face of a common danger, we can forget our smugness for a while and join in the common effort. But soon we forget and go back to our snobbery and our selfishness. The old differences are re-established and the old suspicions are revived. The old poison is spread again and we are once more on the defensive against all who seem to threaten our favored position.

His Kingdom is different. That is the place where we see that the fulfillment of our own best destiny is in being useful to our brethren who need us. If you want to see what the Kingdom means, look at Albert Schweitzer. He is regarded by many as the greatest man of our time. Intellectually, he can hold his own in any circle. He is second to none in interpreting Bach. He is a New Testament scholar and a medical doctor. There is no man more versatile. Yet, with all that power for the gathering of wealth or for the establishing of personal prestige, what does he do? He gives his life to the natives of Africa as a partial repayment for the shameful exploitation they have experienced from the white man.

There is a great story about Schweitzer. He was toiling in the sun alone one day, building his hospital. A native, dressed in a white suit, stood in the shade watching him. When a particularly large timber had to be moved, Dr. Schweitzer asked for some help. But the man refused, saying he had been to school and it was not fitting for an intellectual to work. Dr. Schweitzer smiled. "I used to be an intellectual," he said, "but I couldn't live up to it." Ah, that's it. Until we become citizens of the Kingdom where we are promised an almost absurd kind of joy as we serve our fellows, we shall not attain our real desires. We shall not even continue to live.

Map

Wendell Willkie's phrase "One World" caught on partly because he was a practical man. He was not primarily a churchman or an international dreamer, but a businessman turned politician. The Church had been saying for a long time that in Christ there is no east nor west. Christians have known that maps taking in less than all the human race, are too small.

The map of God's Kingdom is the only one that can guide us in the exploration of the new world. Others may become weary and agree to small boundaries. Others will be willing to mark land beyond our own as jungle, filled with savages. Not so the men who use the map of the Kingdom of God. It is one world because He is one God and we are one family. Whatever the disappointments we may have, and they will be many, the world belongs to God and it is the parish of every Christian. The experience of our time indicates that the one world must be created by men who have the Kingdom's map for their guide. They are the ones who know what will hold us together in spite of much that exists to keep us apart. But even more than that, they know that what everything else fails to do, Jesus Christ can do and does. He can unite us.

We need this Kingdom's map when we explore human relations. It is disturbing to note how we have come to think of personal relations as physical. Cure delinquency by physical exercise; get rid of juvenile criminals by building a few playgrounds; build a church gymnasium and then if there is money left over, build the sanctuary; make marriage a success by teaching young couples physiological harmony; win new adherents to democracy by the judicious use of dollars.

All of this is based on the false premise that men are merely animals and can therefore be manipulated. This is worse than an error—it is a profanation of the holy of holies. Men are spirits. They are finalities and my freedom is limited by every other man's freedom. We are united in God and on no other basis. We find our way through all the intricacies of human relationships only when we use the map of the Kingdom.

It is a paradoxical but profoundly true and important principle of life that the most likely way to reach a goal is to be aiming not at that goal itself but at some more ambitious goal beyond it. This is the meaning . . . of the saying in the New Testament about losing one's life and saving it.[1]

[1] Kuist, *These Words upon Thy Heart*, Knox, 1947, 17.

It is toward that larger goal that we are guided when we follow the map of the Kingdom of God.

Climate

The climate under secularism has grown too cold to produce life. Our success cult has created an atmosphere that has no power to produce greatness. To get on in the world has so penetrated our thinking that we could hardly recognize the monstrous men of our generation for what they were. Hitler cured unemployment and Mussolini made the trains run on time. They simply carried to its logical conclusion the popular, contemporary idea that it makes no difference what you do and how you do it, if you succeed. Once success is achieved, we are convinced that all will be forgiven. Laval and Quisling were representative men produced by this climate. The world is full of that kind of leadership. It is a leadership that deserves the epitaph Clemenceau suggested for a charlatan: "Here lies the body of General Boulanger who died as he lived, a second lieutenant."

The climate of our economic system has been a freezing one for it has tended to place property over men. It will not help much who has control, whether it be management or labor, if that climate remains the same. The machines become too important in our scheme. We build the machine and hire men to tend them. It is better to give the tools to men to be used for men. Only the environment of the Kingdom of God will keep human values bigger in proportion to the machines.

What the Kingdom does for us supremely, is surround us with love. Now we need to purge that word of its Hollywood meanings and go back to the New Testament. It does not mean anything sticky. It means good will. It means seeing men as God sees them. It is the miracle which only the climate of God's Kingdom can produce. A priest who ministered to the feeble-minded was asked how he could stand to be with such poor, slobbering idiots. He replied he had learned to look at their broken minds as God must look at the warped and maimed spirits of all men. Love is seeing men not as they are, but as God sees them.

When Kepler's first marriage failed, he decided to try again on a scientific basis. He listed the qualities of the women he knew whom he considered eligible to be the second Mrs. Kepler. He chose the one who had the most good points in proportion to her bad ones. But the second marriage was also a failure. Then the scientist announced that the problem was unsolvable. But in the meantime, a good many simple people who were not nearly as wise as Kepler, were making successes of their marriages by keeping them in the climate of love.

There is no other answer to our terrifying problems. Love is the law of life and love is the solution of our intolerable tensions. Love is the toughest thing in the world. Love alone has the power to do the mighty works necessary for our salvation. Love is the climate of the Kingdom.

When the two thieves were crucified with Jesus, one of them said in effect, "Do something for us and for yourself. Get us out of this trouble." But the other one rebuked his companion, for as he said, they were being justly punished while Jesus was innocent. Then turning to the center cross, he said, "Jesus, remember me when thou comest in thy kingdom" (Luke 23:42). Do you not see the difference? One man wanted something to be done for him, but the other wanted to be taken into a new climate—a new kingdom. He wanted the mind of Christ. We do not need particular things to be done for us. We need to enter a new life. We need to see at last that God's Kingdom is the real one.

XII

PROVINCE OF THE KINGDOM

> *"Again, the devil taketh him unto an
> exceeding high mountain, and showeth
> him all the kingdoms of the world, and
> the glory of them . . ."* MATTHEW 4:8

One of the most difficult decisions Jesus had to make, was the one concerning his attitude toward this world. Back of the symbolism of the temptation story there was this burning question of what was to be the relation of his kingdom to the kingdoms of the world. It was a difficult question for him and it is for us. The difficulty is due to the fact that Christianity is neither completely this-worldly nor other-worldly. It is both. The Gospel is both in history and beyond history.

We are the kind of creatures who prefer an "either-or" position over a "both-and" situation. At the base of much of our trouble and behind many of our wrong turnings, there is the human tendency to carry things to an extreme. But there are so many things that are right if held in tension by their opposites, which become wrong when they are allowed to go all the way in one direction.

Now let us look at the view which regards Christianity as entirely of this world. This has been the most popular position in our time. There seemed to be such a wide gap between primitive man and civilized man, that many felt we moderns had established a new kingdom on this earth. The similarities between human nature and its beginnings and human nature now were overlooked. If we had come so far, what was to prevent us from going much farther?

This view imprisoned man in the historical process and made him significant only as a member of a group. Out of that belief there came the worship of the nation and the blood. This is still the only faith of millions of people. This is the new Leviathan. This is Moloch risen again. Often a Christian tinge is given to this paganism and a modified Christian vocabulary is used. But it does not worship God.

A great many humanists never expected this emphasis to turn out as it has. They were simply men who became impatient with trying to peer into the mind of God and very often were rebelling against a dogmatic, anthropomorphic theism. To them, the other world seemed in the realm of the unknowable and the unimportant. They were trying to make Christianity work without theology. Many of them were brave liberal spirits who stood for human values against the dehumanizing processes of our industrial society. They wanted Christianity's social concern without its spiritual assumptions.

What is wrong with all of this? Simply that this point of view does not do justice to the relation of each man's separate soul to God. True it is that man is a social creature, but he is not only a social creature. He is made for direct relationship with God, and he knows no rest until he finds it. Unfortunately for this point of view, it is still true that man does not and cannot live by bread alone.

But what about the other extreme which sees our faith as entirely other-worldly? This does violence to the Gospel for it sees the world as completely evil. It intimates that a religious man ought to flee from society and protect himself from its strain. If the world has any meaning, this viewpoint will grant it only a negative one. The world in the mind of other-worldly thinkers, is beyond redemption and must one day be destroyed. But this is certainly a distortion of the Gospel.

We cannot be Christians and doubt the love of God for all His creatures. What shall we do with the affirmation:

> For God so loved the world, that he gave his only
> begotten Son, that whosoever believeth on him should not
> perish, but have eternal life.   JOHN 3:16

We cannot believe that our relations with other men are
merely meaningless, temporary affairs. When we are dealing
with persons, we are dealing with absolutes.

It is true that this world is not enough. But when we
begin to insist that this world is of no importance whatever
—that it is something to endure with what courage we can
muster—we do wrong to the Christian viewpoint. It is like
insisting that since bread will mold if kept too long, it is
bad even when fresh.

Christianity is both this-worldly and other-worldly. The
earth does have significance and God is concerned with it.
His presence can be observed in nature and some of the
deepest religious experiences possible will come to us there.
But this is not the end of the matter. We discover that all
goes wrong with us here if we are not also citizens of heaven.
Arnold Toynbee described the situation as follows:

> On such a view, this world would not be a spiritual exercise
> ground beyond the pale of the Kingdom of God; it would
> be a province of the Kingdom—one province only, and not
> the most important one, yet one which had the same absolute
> value as the rest, and therefore one in which spiritual action
> could, and would, be fully significant and worthwhile; the one
> thing of manifest and abiding value in a world in which all
> other things are vanity.[1]

For the Christian, the world is a province of the Kingdom
of God.

Practicality of Christianity

The thing that really repels many a man from following
Jesus is the practicality of his way. His life is an example

[1] Toynbee, "The Meaning of History for the Soul," *Christianity and
Crisis,* June 23, 1947.

of this characteristic of his teaching. If he had been willing
to withdraw from society and live the contemplative life
only, he never would have been crucified. To all those who
insist that Jesus never meant to interfere in practical affairs,
we need only ask, "Then why did they crucify him?" He
withdrew from time to time, but it was only to let God restore his spirit. He kept coming back and asking pointed
questions, or uncovering the corruption back of so much
pious pretense. If only he had been content to be a priest
instead of a prophet! If only he had not assumed that God
was concerned with motives rather than external action
alone. It was his breaking down the barriers between the
Temple and the market place that worried so many. He
was disturbing.

The teaching of Jesus is full of such practical matters as
money and business. He is not the other-worldly dreamer
who knows nothing about this world's affairs. He knows too
much about them for our comfort. He can tell where the
sin of greed and covetousness finds us. He knows about the
dangers of riches. He is not a believer in the separateness of
what the Pharisee does in the Temple and what he does in
his dealings with his parents. Always he comes to men with a
teaching that confronts us with a practical choice. So often
it is a demand to act now. A man once said he was not too
troubled about the teachings of Jesus he could not understand, but he was very much troubled about the many
things he could understand all too well.

The Bible is the most practical of books. It does not spin
fine theories nor indulge in flights of fantasy. It always has
its feet on the earth and it is speaking directly to some particular problem. That is even true of such books as Daniel
and Revelation. They are to be read in terms of a contemporary historical situation. They are not mechanical fore-
tellings of events in the future, written to provide a field
day for every ingenious dabbler in hidden lore. We may put

our New Testaments on the shelf to gather dust, but they are written to say pointed things about the way we live and the way we ought to live.

What a practical book is the Old Testament. To the Jew, nothing in human experience was foreign to religion. It had to do with diet and cleanliness. It had to do with government and treaties. Always it came back to the need for justice and it judged a people's treatment of widows, orphans, and strangers. The most real thing to Judaism was God. Doubt your neighbor; doubt the sun will rise again; doubt that tomorrow will come—but never doubt God. So the Book that reminded the Jew of this, was his great possession. Israel became the people of a practical Book.

This is why the tyrant is afraid of Christianity. It is not something that will tamely submit to being on a shelf. It will not draw the line and stay behind it. It never can believe that "business is business" or that "politics is politics." The Christian never moves into an experience where he is beyond the reach of his religion's demands.

Jacob Riis came to New York City as an immigrant, and finally started a settlement house supported entirely by free-will gifts. He came to a time when he was out of money, and had to have one hundred and fifty dollars or lose the project. That morning in the mail, two letters arrived and in each letter was a check for seventy-five dollars. The secretary went into an almost superstitious fit of awe. William Riis remembered that his father said to her calmly, "It is the Lord's way. That is the way He works." The point is, Jacob Riis as a Christian, was not surprised that God should see to it the money was made available for His work.

There has been an attempt from time to time since the beginning to make Christianity more complicated. The gnostic heresy is a perennial one and while it comes to us with differing terms, its main argument is always the same. It says there is a special knowledge for the initiated, and a chance to go higher for the speical few. The people who are attracted to the heresy are the consciously superior who cannot believe that the common saint is fit company for them. But the Church has rightly branded all such teaching as false. The Gospel does not need a certain intelligence before it can be understood. It is a plain way for any plain man. It demands honesty, but most of all, it demands people who are willing to be led in a straight path, and who will not despise the presence of God in the common places. Christianity is a promise for men who are not up to esoteric speculation, but who want practical help in living.

The Earth Is the Lord's

The world in which we live has the marks of God. One cannot but be impressed with the delicate balance which science reveals everywhere. Whenever we try to ignore that, we get into trouble. The world becomes a barren desert for those who forget its laws, but if men remember the laws and obey them, it is a storehouse. When DDT was used indiscriminately to get rid of troublesome insects, it got rid of some needed insects as well. The end result was worse than the situation at the beginning. The earth cannot be treated without understanding or respect.

We have seen what happens in vast sections of our country when we mine the land. If we upset the balance for the sake of profits, we bequeath to our children dustbowls. If we cut the forests without discrimination or replanting, we have floods. We cannot do as we please except within limitations. When we cease to love the earth, it will no longer serve us.

The same thing is true of human society. There are laws to be maintained and a balance to guard. There is a growing concern over the problem of our big, sprawling metropolises. The city's blind greed and lust for wealth and bigness, creates breeding places for crime and delinquency. The same thing happens when a society is built on slavery. The slave becomes not the foundation of such a society, but its fifth column. We are never free to organize our life just as we please. There is a higher power which has set limitations for us.

The human characteristic is to decide first of all what we want and then insist upon getting it no matter what the cost or result may be. A great number of people go through their whole lives finding fault with others and getting increasingly bitter toward life, because they cannot have what they want. It would be wiser to find out if what they want is possible, and if it is, how much it will cost. Christianity is always telling us that we must come to terms with the way things are. The earth is the Lord's, which means that whatever is displeasing to Him, is destructive for us. We have to come to terms with the world and not believe that because we are good, special favors will be granted to us. He makes the rain to fall both on the just and on the unjust.

A little boy in a Christian school in India was facing his first examination. Because he had been taught that he should always pray before undertaking any venture, he said this prayer: "O God, help me to pass my examinations. Help my classmates to pass their examinations. Help the whole school to pass. Help the whole world to pass." That was a good prayer, for it assumed that the whole world stands under the examination of God and must meet His testings.

The world is a province of the Kingdom. Says the 24th Psalm:

> The earth is the Lord's and the fulness thereof; the world, and they that dwell therein.
> For he hath founded it upon the seas, and established it upon the floods. 1, 2

We cannot even feed ourselves unless we remember that. In his study of natural resources, Professor Mather of Harvard University came to the conclusion that there was enough and to spare if the world was one. Trouble comes when some get too much and refuse others their rightful part. No nation can be self-supporting, in spite of the attempts made in that direction to prepare for war. When we begin to think of our ownership of the earth instead of His, everything goes wrong. For peace to be a lasting reality, we must submit to the insight of the Psalmist, that the earth is the Lord's and not ours.

If this seems to have a forbidding sound, it also has a word of encouragement and promise. Everything does not depend on us. The beginning of a long and difficult day is almost too much to face the first thing in the morning. A man was told that to develop his character he should do at least one thing each day he did not want to do. He replied, "I do. I get up." But the tasks of the day are done one at a time. To the man who will begin, God apportions power enough for the doing. The young preacher who draws back in horror at the idea of forty-eight sermons to be preached this year and every year of his life, soon learns that it is a matter of one at a time, and God gives him more to say than he can find time to say. The earth is the Lord's, and the tasks which the world demands of us are not too difficult, for they come from Him.

What a tragedy it is when a man begins to think of his work as outside the province of the Kingdom of God. We fall into the trap of believing that some work may be sacred, but other work is secular. That the preacher should expect help in doing his work well, we can believe. That the plumber should expect the same help from God, seems to us profane. But if a man's work is his greatest contribution to the Kingdom, he ought to expect divine help in being a good plumber. I have never forgotten a sermon I heard Leslie Weatherhead preach in City Temple, London, the year before the war. He took ordinary jobs and presented them as co-operative adventures with God. No one who heard that sermon could ever see his work as anything but a high calling.

This is the secret of Paul's joyous abandonment. None of us will ever face a more difficult or seemingly hopeless job than his. But so sure was he that the earth was God's, he never doubted strength would be given for the task. Its ultimate outcome was in the hands of his Lord. The cure for much of the neurotic fearfulness which stamps our efforts, is a new realization that we are dwelling in a province of the Kingdom and our work is not just our own.

Some years ago, an Italian company built the two fastest ships afloat. They held the speed record between Genoa and New York. But their bows had been made so sharp the ships rolled at high speed and were in danger of turning over. Then the engineers built stabilizers which threw their weight on the side where a balance was needed. They held the ships steady and kept them safe, even at high speeds and in severe storms. God is the world's stabilizer. He keeps it steady, for it belongs to Him. It is this consciousness which keeps us confident, even when others have yielded to their fears.

Stewardship

The fine concept of stewardship has been neglected by Christians to their detriment. It is much more than tithing, though that is part of it. Stewardship is a philosophy of living and a broad program of giving. It means that we do not own anything here, but are called on to administer our possessions in the name of the Owner. All of our lives will be affected when touched by this spirit. The freedom that it brings, is one of the great experiences of Christianity. It brings us the joy of giving.

The futility of hoarding becomes plain to any thinking man. Why should we pile up perishable goods like a squirrel? Who wants to have happen to him what happens to the miser? I have never seen a man bent on collecting goods, that I did not want to say in the words of Jesus: "Woe unto you rich." No sensitive man envies such as these, but feels, on the contrary, a pity at this waste of living. A man went to a wealthy citizen to obtain a gift for a community project. He was refused on the grounds that the man simply could not afford to give anything at this particular time. "Joe," said the solicitor as he prepared to leave, "if you are not careful, you are going to be the richest man in our cemetery." Is that a worthy goal for a thinking man?

In contrast to that, I think of my father. He never had much money and at no time did he have an adequate financial margin. Yet at one of his lowest periods I saw him give a man a dollar. When I remonstrated with him, his answer was, "It came out of my tithe. Of course I could afford it." But I knew many a man who was a hundred times better off financially who would not have been able to afford it.

When a man becomes a steward, he looks at things from a new point of view. The Hazen Foundation has a little pamphlet with this intriguing title: *Teaching Economics with a Sense of the Infinite and the Urgent*. Can the dreary science be taught with that sense? Yes, for everything can be observed from the viewpoint of the eternal. Jesus commands us to think of treasure in heaven and not on earth. The Christian steward is the man who has learned to think of his earthly treasures in the light of treasures in heaven.

Giving is an art to be learned. In some ways, it is unfortunate that we are not born with it. Our first impulse is to get and keep. We want to fight off any who may come asking us to share. Many a man never gets beyond this stage. If he is hounded, he may give a niggardly check. But giving is always painful and only polite blackmail will separate him from his possessions. It is a sad truth that the churches are full of people who have never been taught what Jesus meant when he said, "It is more blessed to give than to receive." This is really tragic, and it is an indication of one of the worst failures of Christian education.

Consider the sponge and the spring. A sponge swells up several times its normal size in order to hold on to all it can absorb. The only way to get anything out of it, is to squeeze it. But the spring is always giving out. It does not keep anything back but spills out across the meadow with abandonment. The sponge is a corpse, but the spring is alive. Men die when they keep, and the light goes out when they no longer enjoy their giving.

It is not only a matter of giving money. There are our talents and our time. The steward knows that if he wants to administer what has been committed unto him, he cannot bury his talent in the earth. The sense of having to use what we have, redeems us from self-pity and gives us a sense of the dignity of our lives. Maltbie Babcock wrote:

> Genuine kindness oftenest comes from self-repression, a cheerful message from a sad soul, a brave word from a trembling heart, a generous gift from a slender purse, a helping hand from a tired man. It is not your mood, but the other man's need, that determines kindness.

Stewardship is a kind of insurance against selfishness and narrowness. It is the only assurance we have that in dealing with secular things, we will not become personally secularized.

World's Impermanence

People who look upon the world as the end of all things, have trouble keeping up their courage in the face of crumbling hopes and defeated aims. Why is everything so impermanent? Why can't we build something that will last? It is no wonder that in the face of the destruction of time, many a Christian looks to the other world entirely. Optimistic humanism always ends in despair because its hopes are always betrayed. Utopia may seem to be just around the corner, but it fades before us like the end of the rainbow. The worldling is always sure that a few more changes will bring about the beloved community. He believes that if we kill a few more thousand people, we can establish peace. But when at last he loses his hope that human efforts can establish the good life here, he becomes of all men most miserable. He often swings from the extreme left to the extreme right.

In his famous *History of the Persian Wars*, Herodotus comments:

> The cities which were formerly great have most of them become insignificant; and such as are at present powerful, were weak in olden times. I shall, therefore, discourse equally of both, convinced that prosperity never continues long in one place.

Now at first sight, this is a devastating picture of life in the world. Weary souls whose paths have seemed to wind uphill always, hope for a resting place where they may find release from their exertions. The dispossessed, fighting for their rights, hope to create a society where the fight is over and the victory won. The man who is tempted almost beyond his power to resist, dreams of achieving a character impervious to temptation. We make our sacrifices in the hope of a time when the lights will come on and the darkness be ended forever. To say to such as these that there is no permanent victory and there can be none, seems like announcing the futility of all striving.

But it is not so. The universe is built on the principle of growth, and it is more necessary for us to grow than it is for us to be comfortable. Men are rightly suspicious of anything which hints at the stagnation of perfection, or suggests a changeless future. That is why Methodists have always had to be careful in explaining what they do not mean by John Wesley's doctrine of Christian perfection. If it meant that men could achieve a state in which they no longer needed forgiveness and judgment, it was not acceptable.

One of the reasons young people are not particularly thrilled with the idea of becoming saints, is because in their minds, the saint is one who has achieved perfection and hence can no longer grow. Yet Paul addressed his First Corinthian Letter to those "called to be saints" at Corinth. But were they saints in the sense of being perfect? Read the Letter and you will discover that they were worse than average church members of today. Paul knew that, but to him, a saint was a man who was moving in a certain direction, not a man who had arrived. He was not a man who had achieved or already been made perfect, but one who pressed forward.

Are we then completely at the mercy of time? Is there no resting place down here? The Christian faith knows that each man's soul can be invincible and that the victories and the defeats which really matter are within. A man is always affected by his environment. It is for him an important fact, but it is not the essential fact. The Christian is in the world, but he is not necessarily of the world. There is set within each of us an inner fortress which none may enter unless he opens the gate. Every man has the final advantage over force for he can always say no. This is a rock upon which we stand.

We live in a world that can be either too important or not important enough. It can be something which enslaves us or something which repels us. It can be for us a prison or it can be a fool's paradise. It will put its mark on us. No matter how spiritual may be our desires, we must still use material things. The secularist has no satisfactory answer to his problem. Neither has the other-worldly dreamer. But for the Christian, the world is neither frightening nor enslaving. It is under the loving rule of God. Possessions are to be administered in His name. In the midst of the impermanence of the world, God has established man's eternal soul, and He has made man's spirit undefeatable.

Handel wrote his "Messiah" in twenty-four days. Critics say that perhaps this has never been equaled as a record for great musical composition. He hardly left the house during that time. His servant said oftentimes he would take a meal up, put it on the table, and come back an hour later to find it untouched. When the servant came into the room after Handel had finished Part Two, which contains the Hallelujah Chorus, he saw the composer looking out of the window, tears shining in his eyes. Said he, "I did think I did see all Heaven before me, and the great God Himself." It is this which the Christian sees shining through the world. This province of His Kingdom is marked with the glory of our God. The Christian mind knows how to live in the world and be free.

XIII

BOOK OF LIFE

> *"And these words, which I command thee this day, shall be upon thy heart . . ."*
>
> DEUTERONOMY 6:6

Someday I want to write a book about the Bible. This is not because I have some special knowledge to share or some particular information to give. Men who have dedicated their lives to the ministry of the Church have to give up the idea of being specialized scholars. The critical books about the Bible should be left to the scholars. But there is a desire within me to bear witness in a personal testimony as to what the Bible means to me. It is the same desire that comes to a Christian in a prayer meeting. He wants to testify concerning God's goodness. For when I think of what the Book means to me, it is too good to keep.

My personal experience with the Bible may be worth sketching briefly because it is the story of drifting away from it and then finding the road back. The Bible was my parents' book. We had family worship and there comes to me yet the picture of the worn volume which my father took from the table after breakfast and read with a careful kind of dignity. In Sunday School, we heard Bible stories and learned Bible verses. I wish it could be said there came to me then a sincere affection for the Book, but that would not be true. No one ever tried to convince us that the Bible was anything but a special, somewhat peculiar, Book, for special occasions.

I read the Bible through in my early teens as a kind of penance and protection. It was not a very enjoyable experience. There was much that made little sense to me. There were chapters of endless lists of names which seemed necessary to read, of course, but added nothing to my enjoyment or my wisdom. There was a kind of virtuous feeling that I was doing something praiseworthy and religious. A captain of a Civil War company decreed that every man indulging in profanity should read one chapter from the Bible. One private reported that he read "all of Genesis and Exodus and starting Leviticus, and had a fine prospect of finishing the Old Testament before his three month enlistment expired." Our modern religious education is certainly on the right track when it tries to take the element of penance out of Bible study.

My first introduction to a liberal interpretation of the Scriptures came in college. It was a rather upsetting ex-

perience. To treat the Bible as if it was subject to the critical judgment of scholars like any ordinary book, seemed a
little sacrilegious. I was attracted and repelled. There was
no doubt in my mind but that it certainly sounded reasonable to doubt Moses' authorship of the first five books of
the Bible, and Paul's responsibility for Hebrews. Neverthe-
less, it seemed to take away a great deal of the Bible's
authority. My father did not help much when I talked it
over with him. In his mind, the whole thing was of the
devil and he could not see how a church college had such
courses in its curriculum.

There followed what may best be called the smart-aleck
period. It was a time of posing as an idol-smashing intellectual. One leaned over backward in drawing the contrast
between fundamentalism and modernism (curious how the
very terms sound archaic to me now). We were not too sure
what we did believe, but we knew what we did not believe.
It seemed better to be honest and intelligent, than to be
mistaken and good. The Bible was treated in a high-handed
manner as if it had been provided for a background to our
brilliance. We learned to dispute authorship and dates.

This was the time when much objection was raised to
Bible-centered teaching materials in the church school.
Children should be taught about the birds and the bees,
but not about the child Samuel or the boy Jesus. A college
girl once confessed to her professor that she knew nothing
about the Bible because she had attended one of those
modern Sunday schools. The Book seemed to have passed
its day.

But there has come a change in my experience and I believe in the thinking of liberal Protestantism. Gradually it
has dawned upon us, that after you have disposed of the
question as to when a book in the Bible was written and
who wrote it, you still have to answer the question: Is it
true? Facing the dark experiences of our time, we began

to discover that the words of insight and encouragement we needed were in the Bible. Under the impact of our cynicism and fear, the Book began to shine in a new light. It spoke to our deepest needs. After it threshed the chaff out of the materialistic wheat, it revealed how little nourishment we had been getting from contemporary philosophy. In a way that we had never experienced before, the Bible became to us our Book of Life.

There is no cause to regret the time and energy spent on Biblical criticism. It has cleared away a good deal of the underbrush and burned up much trash. It has made the Book more alive and more vital. When one compares the narrow spirit of sectarianism so characteristic of the Inerrancy-Worshipers, he thanks God that he has been lead beyond that impasse. For now he is no longer rushing to the defense of the Bible. He knows that it needs no defense and that nothing true is opposed to it. The Bible becomes a freedom road and reading it is a spiritual adventure.

Christians today have an opportunity their fathers never had, when it comes to using the Book. There is a vast amount of new knowledge available to any thinking man who wants to take it. Reading the Bible can be one of the most thrilling projects anyone ever undertook. There are commentaries and introductions and reading guides easily obtainable. There is background material to give the books their historical and social settings. What a tragedy it is that just at this time, there are still so many Bible illiterates!

The infant Thomas Babington Macaulay was playing with a little girl who began to take the pebbles he had used to mark off the boundaries of his play garden. Angrily he piped: "Cursed be Sallie, for it is written 'Cursed be he that removeth his neighbor's landmark.' "[1] It is a fine thing to have the Bible ever at one's command, not only in anger,

[1] Nelson, *Our Roving Bible*, Abingdon-Cokesbury, 1945, 90.

but in sorrow or joy. It always has the word we need to hear.

What It Is Not

The Bible is one of the best examples of Jesus' word: ". . . and a man's foes shall be they of his own household" (Matthew 10:36). Ill-advised champions have done it much harm by making it into something it is not.

For one thing, the Bible is not an end in itself. The one thing most dangerous about overemphasizing the memorization of the Scriptures, is the assumption that memorizing without understanding is virtuous. There is really no more value in memorizing the Ten Commandments or the Beatitudes than there is in memorizing the multiplication table, unless the Commandments and the Beatitudes demand and receive a personal response. Because words happen to be written in the Bible, does not give them power to automatically produce character if they are learned by rote. Words that do not change life have little value wherever they may be found.

A friend of mine was taught the books of the Bible from Genesis to Revelation. It is a great help, as he tells me, when it comes to looking up a reference. He knows that Romans will not be found among the Prophets. But it is doubtful that this memorizing ever made him a better man or helped him to live more courageously. There are persons who throw out proof texts as if any word anywhere in the Bible is a proof of any argument on any subject. All of this is magical nonsense and does the Book much harm.

We must always remember that our faith is built around a Person and not around a Book. We find truth through the personality of Jesus. When Protestantism was born it did not intend that we should substitute for the intolerable authority of an ecclesiastical institution the dogmatic authority of a Book. The Bible leads us to life and illuminates

cur pathway, but it does nothing for us until we appropri-
ate its truth.

The Bible did not create the religious community of
Israel nor of Christians. It was the other way around. The
community produced the Book. That is to say that the
authority of the Bible is the authority of life and experience. It is the record of God dealing with men and the
story of people living together with God.

One of the most amazing things for us to contemplate is
the way God gave people, no better than we are, the mighty
insights of the Scriptures. We learn that life then was very
much the same as life now, in spite of surface differences.
Yet out of that life there came the Patriarchs, the Prophets,
the Apostles, the Saints. Out of Israel's life there came Jesus
Christ. God does not draw up an ideal situation and send
it down from above. He dwells with men just as they are
with no special advantages, and they create a community.
The Bible is a story of the community and the fellowship,
for it came up out of that setting.

Augustine St. Clare was speaking of his mother to his
cousin:

> The Bible was my mother's Book. By it she lived and died.
> . . . Why Cousin, that mother has been all that has stood
> between me and utter unbelief for years. She was a direct em-
> bodiment and personification of the New Testament, a living
> fact to be accounted for, and to be accounted for in no other
> way than by its truth.[2]

The Bible becomes a two-way passage. It came out of the
life of the community, but it becomes a creative force giving
back to the Church and individuals, insights and inspiration for further growth.

The Bible is not a textbook of medicine or science or
history. If it were not so serious, it would be amusing to
watch the number of young people who go out from our

[2] Kuist, *op. cit.*, 24.

Christian homes and churches to college, and there lose their religion. One wants to ask what kind of religion they were taught that is so easily lost. True enough, many of them come back again on a firmer foundation, but too many of them never recapture the spiritual power they once had. What is the cause of this waste?

In the majority of cases, the trouble is due to a misconception of what the Bible is. They have been taught that it is the guide not only for spiritual truth, but for scientific truth. When they are confronted with modern scientific teaching, they know that it is in conflict with what they were taught in Sunday school. Under the false impression that it is all or nothing, they choose what seems to them truth in science, and they throw overboard all the Bible. Or they may find it difficult to adjust some of the historical material to a critical study of those times. Or if disease is caused only by evil spirits, they ask, what about all that medical knowledge has discovered about the laws of health?

Most of this might be spared our young people if it were plainly stated that the Bible is a textbook of religion, of the eternal spiritual truth of God that is unchanging, and of life. But it is not an authority on these other matters. The men who wrote the Bible were the men of their own day and they believed in the science of their day. Nearly all of us have accepted that truth, within limitations at least. There are not many people (though there are still a few) who believe that the world is flat because the Old Testament seems to have that view of it. Even the literalists have to pick and choose what they will take literally. We would do well to state frankly that we do not expect any young person or old person to take his knowledge about the physical universe from the Bible.

This is of no great matter anyway. We can take the science out of the Bible and we have lost nothing. Its essential message is unimpaired. What men may think about the shape of the world is not too significant, but what they think about their destiny is. If we have made progress in the realm of diagnosing and healing disease since the New Testament was closed, let us rejoice. We are still in need of its wisdom about spirits sick with sin.

The American historian, David S. Muzzey, challenged the Christian emphasis on Jesus in these words:

> Imagine a modern lecturer in medicine or a demonstrator in the laboratory having to begin with a prayer to Aescupalius, and then confine his exposition to a commentary on Galen, trying to show how the ideas of the Greek physician two millenniums ago are still and always will be true, because divinely revealed. Yet this is what goes on essentially in many a pulpit today.[3]

The blindness here is the inability to note the difference between scientific truth and religious truth. Science changes and is quickly out of date. Spiritual understanding is eternal. But if we insist that the science of the Bible is authoritative for Christians, then we would be wide open to Professor Muzzey's attack.

Let us get over the absurd idea that all of the Bible is on the same level. The foolishness of opening the Book at any page and finding guidance for the day, springs from this misconception of the nature of the Biblical Books. The Bible has its high peaks and its valleys. It has its chapters of marvelous vision, and its chapters of endless genealogies. To read the Bible with a dull willingness to plod through every chapter, is to develop a dislike for the Book and miss the whole point of its witness.

Surely anyone can see that Mark and John do not have the same picture of Jesus. Is James to be put on the same level as Philippians? Is Leviticus of equal value with Isaiah? Just to ask such questions reveals the crime of the levelers.

[3] Lichliter, *Whose Leaf Shall Not Wither,* Abingdon-Cokesbury, 1946, 76.

The Bible can speak only to those who are able to hear and we will judge the Books in relation to their ability to speak to us. Probably it is the other way around and the Bible is judging us. The point is that our favorite books are the ones that find us.

All of these false views of the Bible are attempts to limit it. We want to make it a guide to a closed system of life, and it will not work. The Bible is the Book of freedom and when these limitations are cast off, it becomes able to do its great work for men.

What the Bible Is

The Bible is a great awakener. No other book has such power to bring new ideas and new thoughts into men's minds. Robert Frost said to a group of students, "I am not a teacher, but an awakener." That of course is the best kind of teaching. It is what the Bible does supremely. This power of the Book never seems to wane. The man who reads it for the first time is at once impressed with the freshness of its insights. So is the man who has read it for a long lifetime.

I never read over the Sermon on the Mount without feeling as if a fresh breeze is blowing through my life. The dull atmosphere of routine and boredom is blown away. In its place, there comes an exhilarating sense of the wonder and miracle of life. To the Hebrew mind, the world was full of the awe of God and this Hebrew Book has the same sense of awe shining through all its pages. To a tired generation, Bible reading would be the best tonic available.

One of the arguments for the superiority of the religious life is its adventurousness. Strangely enough a people with every reason to sink into the slough of despondency, refuses to do so as long as faith is maintained. The record of the Jews is enough to give inspiration to any people whose God is the Lord. They had tribulation and persecution, but they were not beaten down to dullness. The Bible is a story of how God restores the souls of His chosen with a vision of the new earth.

The Bible is an awakener to the danger of sin. Whenever men get too confident of their own goodness, it is a sure sign that they are not the people of the Book. No one who reads the Bible is able to forget his need of salvation. Sin is such a positive force in the story that it is personified. Only when we cut ourselves off from this history do we forget what happens to men because of their pride. It is a great thing to keep oneself alert to this danger. The Bible is like a sentinel standing guard over against our tendency to take evil too lightly.

This is an eternal book, of course, and is simply dateless. The eternal drama of man's search for God and of God's search for man is here put into its imperishable form. This is an unchanging subject and yet because it is always new to every man, it is the freshest subject there is. Compare it with other literature and you cannot help but see the difference. The modern best sellers come and go like so many feverish dreams. But the Bible is reality for it has explored the depths of the human comedy.

If we had more knowledge of the Bible, we would not be so easily swayed by propaganda. It is the empty soul and mind which is ready to embrace all extreme opinion. It is the faithless generation that is ready to listen to the siren calls of dictators. When men know something about life in the image of God, they have a standard of judgment, and a safeguard against the fads which so easily beset us and deceive us. This Book has gone through the testing of the years and suffered the hammering blows of every competing way of life. It is a judgment on all private and public policy.

A friend once suggested that a church could do a great service to a community if it would set against the contem-

porary voices, the word of the Bible. His idea was that a
sign showing what some politician said and then what the
Bible said about the same question, would be most enlight-
ening. He had a point, but it would be much better if we
knew our Bible well enough to do that for ourselves.
Blessed is the man who asks about every suggested course of
action, "How does this appear in the light of the Scriptures?"

The world's reaction to the Bible is similar to that of
Lord Lyndhurst's reactions to testimony. His lips would
often seem to move yet no sound could be heard coming
from them. But the registrar beneath him could hear the
Judge mutter, "What a fool that man is!" Then after a
little while he would say, "Not such a fool as I thought."
And then after another interval he might mutter, "Egad, it
is I that was the fool."[4] This has been the reaction of the
world to the Bible. First of all it wants to say, "What utter
foolishness and what a quaint idea." But as time goes on,
we turn back to the Book with the sad confession that if
we had listened to it, we would have been saved. We are
the fools, not the Bible.

The Bible is a workable book. Learned men of all kinds
are apt to fall into the use of a jargon to express their ideas.
Sometimes it seems as if one of the rules for writing philosophy is to make it as obscure as possible and never use simple language if complicated terms can be found. The plain
speech of the Bible is one of its greatest characteristics.
Oliver Wendell Holmes, Jr. said that any two philosophers
could tell each other all they know in two hours. But they
spend a lifetime and use a dozen long volumes to do it.
How compact and straightforward is the Bible.

Take the Joseph story in the last thirteen chapters of
Genesis for an example. Thomas Mann used that as a

---

[4] Curtis and Greenslet, *The Practical Cogitator,* Houghton Mifflin,
1945, 407.

framework for his great trilogy consisting of four volumes. Granted that he expands it and allows his artistic imagination to recreate it. Yet after reading Mann's work, and finding parts of it a little tedious and drawn out, I came to the conclusion that the Bible's appeal is partly its austere style. After I have waded through the volumes of the mystics, it always seems to me that Jesus, St. John, and St. Paul said what the mystics were trying to say, only they said it with directness and simplicity.

The Bible can never get far away from the practical affairs of life. The Old Testament is dealing with the social life of a people. The New Testament is talking about the personal relations between men and God and between men and men. The historical books have the purpose of interpreting the past so that men may learn how to live in the future with wisdom. The prophetic books are not divine fortune telling manuals, but interpreters of Israel's life in the light of the purposes of God. The Gospels are written for the encouragement and guidance of Christians. Paul writes his Letters because he cannot be everywhere at the same time and he must deal with the practical problems of his mission. Even a book like Hebrews with its Platonic philosophy, is defined as a "word of exhortation" by the author (13:22). Revelation is a message of encouragement to suffering Christians and a call to faithfulness.

It is one of the chief purposes of the Bible to help men keep first things first. It is a Book that keeps our eyes on the center of life. Dean Wicks of Princeton says that his children found an old recording of a Beethoven sonata and bored an off-center hole in it. When it was played on the phonograph, it made a screeching din of the Beethoven music. Life that is lived off-center may have some interesting qualities, but the general effect is discord and futility. Only when we keep God at the center, says the Bible, will we be able to produce the music of harmony and triumph.

However, we must say also that the Bible is a dangerous book. What a strange thing it seems now to read of the public notices posted in England at the time of Henry VIII. They said:

> No women, nor artificers, nor apprentices, journeymen, serving-men, yeomen, husbandmen or laborers shall read the Bible in English to himself or another, privately or openly on pain of a month's imprisonment.

In a day when we try to encourage everyone to read the Bible, how can we explain this fear of it?

The Catholic Church has never gotten over its reluctance to see the Bible unrestrictedly circulated in the language of the people. It prevented it for as long as possible. Protestantism, on the other hand, has sent out an ever-widening stream of Bibles all over the earth, for one of its foundations is the open Bible. We must confess that when we see the weird way some sects use the Bible, we can sympathize with the position of our Catholic brethren. Yet we believe that in spite of the dangers involved, the open Bible has been one of the greatest civilizing forces in history. Nations have built their laws on it. Societies have been molded by it. Democracy stands on it. One of the best indications of its power is the way tyranny fears it and burns it.

But the Bible is dangerous for any man to read. Give it an inch and it takes a yard. It is a mirror of man's life and a judgment on his motives. It has a penetrating power that goes through our defenses. It is destructive of illusions. Like a surgeon's knife, it plunges into our selfishness. It sears and dries up the mildew of the heart. It smashes self-pity. And more important than all, it brings me face to face with God without any institution or priest in between. It takes courage to read the Bible—the courage to expose one's life to God.

The Bible is the Word of God in a way that no other

writing is or can be. This is not to say that it is a collection
of rules defining our relationship to Him, but rather it is
the creation of an environment where His spirit can act
upon us directly. When the early commentators called the
Greek of the New Testament the "Greek of the Holy
Spirit," they spoke more wisely than they knew. For while
it turned out to be the Greek of the common man, it was
truly the language of the Holy Spirit, which is always plain
enough for any man to understand.

We may believe that the Bible should be subjected to
criticism like any other writing and measured by the same
criteria used to judge any great piece of literature. But any
man who has followed the process to its conclusion, cannot
escape the assurance that here is a Holy Book. This is the
great thing about the critical approach—it strengthens
faith instead of weakening it. That God could use men and
lead them to write down such things as are found in the
Bible, lifts up the heart anew. We study it and say with
Jacob, "Surely the Lord is in this place, and I knew it not"
(Genesis 28:16).

No man ever had a deeper sense of this truth about the
Bible than George Adam Smith. It has been said that while
noise in his classroom never disturbed him if he was lecturing, woe unto any student who made the slightest noise when
he was reading the Bible. One time when lecturing before
a group of ministers, he read a Biblical passage with such
effect that they broke into applause. Professor Smith became white with anger. "Gentlemen," he said with inten-
sity, "we accept God's word. We do not approve it."

It is this quality which sets the Bible apart from any
other literature. We approve other writings or disapprove
them. But there is something about the Bible which makes
our taking this liberty seem a blasphemy. It is to be inscribed on our hearts and remembered. It is too far beyond
us to make our little judgments anything but presumptu-

ous. We do not judge it, but the Bible judges us. Modern as we may become, we are still far behind the Book. Other writings may grow old, but fresh as each new morning, God's Word appears unto each new generation. It is the written word most effective in creating the mind of Christ.

XIV

THE GOSPEL AS THE ANSWER

"Rejoice in the Lord always: again I will say, Rejoice."
PHILIPPIANS 4:4

A Presbyterian student preacher discovered one Sunday morning that the only way he could reach his church, was to ice skate down the river. After the morning service, the elders called him into private conference. They were deeply shocked that a minister of the Gospel should break the Sabbath by skating. The young man explained the circumstances and they considered it gravely. Finally they asked him if he had enjoyed skating down the river, and when he assured them he had not, they decided it was permissible.

This emphasis on the Gospel as something dour and forbidding, is not so prevalent now as it once was. Not many people today make Sunday a miserable day for their children. Not many of us fast or wear hair shirts. As a matter of fact, it would be a good thing for some of us if we did. But a very great number of people think of the Gospel as narrowing. We remember Jesus' word:

Enter ye in by the narrow gate: for wide is the gate, and broad is the way, that leadeth to destruction, and many are they that enter in thereby. For narrow is the gate, and straitened the way, that leadeth unto life, and few are they that find it.   MATTHEW 7:13-14

A generation that has worshiped tolerance as a way of life, will be suspicious of anything suggesting narrowness. We have made of our iconoclasm a cult. We have talked much about a person's right to personal fulfillment. We have meant that doing what we want to do when we want to do it is more important than fulfilling our obligations. This often involves hurting other people and breaking promises. But it can be justified if we assume the primary right is individual pleasure.

Now the Gospel will have nothing to do with that philosophy. It will ask where we got the idea we have a right to consider only ourselves. Who said so? In what book is it to be found? For Christianity, there are many things more important than my selfish desires. An easygoing, soft, tolerant viewpoint it hates. It has nothing but scorn for a way of life based on pleasure as an end in itself.

Yet Christians have not found Christianity a black and cheerless way. They have found it the realization of their deepest needs. One of the themes that runs through Paul's Letters is joy. He can be writing to a church split apart with bickering and rivalry and suddenly break into the greatest poem about love ever written. Jesus speaks of the state of blessedness to be experienced by those who are hungry and cold and poor.

A boy who had been on the frontier suffering its dangers and privations came home to his brother's farm for a visit. When the older brother urged the boy to stay, he refused because he said that farming was hard work. "But what is trapping but hard work? What about fear of Indians and cold and hunger?" asked the farmer. "Well," said the boy, "we never counted it work." And nothing is work unless you would rather be doing something else. What may seem like sacrifice and privation to the outsider, is the fulfillment of life for the Christian. He talks not at all about sacrifice. In the light of what Christ means to him, he never made a sacrifice in his life. The Gospel is joy.

Conspiracy of Goodness

For one thing, the Gospel is the answer to our human need for adventure. We are not content with mere safety and the most dissatisfied people in the world are those who have made themselves as safe as possible and killed all willingness to risk for a purpose. One of the reasons we have carnivals is to provide people with an artificial thrill. Nervous breakdowns and neuroses do not come, as a rule, to people who struggle to make both ends meet. They come to the people whose warfare seems to be past.

G. K. Chesterton with his characteristic insight, once said, "Morality is the most dark and daring of conspiracies." The good life is always the daring life and the Christian life always has the thrill of high adventure. It is evil that is boring and it is sin that is dull. In spite of the pagan's attempt to make sin alluring, it always puts its gray color over everything it touches. In contrast, the Gospel is a brilliant excitement.

Civilization is adventurous, not savagery. When men try to make the human experiment climb, they start developing the spirit of culture. The savage is willing to live like an intelligent animal with no high hopes or plans. The conflict between the farmer and the hunter runs through most history of the beginnings of civilization. The hunter seems like a free fellow in comparison with the farmer who settles in one place. But it is the farmer who has decided to do something about the slavery imposed on him by nature.

The dictator often romanticizes himself in comparison with the matter-of-fact ways of democracy. But it is democracy that represents adventure. It is willing to risk an ex-

periment where men govern themselves and decide their
own policies. The tyrant is a throw-back to primitive times
when a man with a big club lorded it over weaker men.

The good citizen is the man with a sense of adventure,
not the criminal. It is society that represents the big chance.
Who first dared to believe that men could live together
under law and thus free themselves for the more important
tasks? It was an idea so big and so dangerous, that he must
have been of heroic stature. The criminal is the coward who
tries to halt the procession. He is the one who would prevent the real rebels from having their chance.

Marriage is another case in point. It is too bad we teach
our children to believe that the Hollywood practicers of
polygamy represent romance and excitement. They are
merely spoiled adolescents—the eternal adolescents—who
never have been able to attain emotional maturity. Monog-
amy is one of the most revolutionary things humanity ever
attempted. What happens when two people decide to build
a home? They set forth on an adventure so fraught with
danger that one sometimes wonders how anyone ever dares
to undertake it. So many things can go wrong and so many
uncertainties lurk in the future. But at the beginning, some
of our ancestors decided the promised values were so great,
it ought to be tried. What a dark and daring conspiracy the
home and marriage is!

The evil life is always the cowardly life for it is the easy
way. We have done much in our time to understand the
environment of criminals. We have learned that certain
conditions are more productive of crime than others. Like
every truth, we often carry it too far. We conclude that nobody is to blame for anything. If a person is a criminal,
don't blame him but blame his parents, or his neighborhood. But it will not do! There is still an element of choice
and the criminal is a man who has chosen the short cut
because it seemed to him the easy way.

There are very few of us who can justify our evil by assuring ourselves we could not help it. The eternal conflict between the champions of free will and the believers in determinism never can be settled on the intellectual plane. You can make about as good a case logically for one as you can for the other. The conflict is settled on the plane of experience. We make choices, and no clever arguments can justify our choice of evil. We know when we took the easy way—which is to say, the cowardly way.

The evil life is the reactionary life. It is the evil man who stands in the way of progress. Every step forward taken by the race has been an overcoming of the lethargy of evil. It is illustrated in the case of the alcoholic. He is not a free, adventurous spirit, but an enslaved spirit. He illustrates James Martineau's remark that the man who has sunk into habitual evil, "has lost the privilege of sin and sunk away from the ranks of persons into the destiny of things."

Christians sometimes sink into this same despondency when they assume their faith has provided them with a finality and a permanent resting place here. There is a sense in which the Kingdom of God "is as a man traveling." We need not fear the difficulty of our tasks ahead, but we need to fear that we may no longer rise to meet them with courage. We may sulk in our tent like Saul, when we ought to be with David on the field. We may be holding on to an old truth which served its day but now stands as a barrier to the future. This is not where the joy of the saints is to be found.

Goodness is a rebellious thing and the early Christians found themselves marked as rebels. They were those who were turning the world upside down. It has been a long time since many people spoke that way about Christians. But when they do say that, you know they are speaking of those gallant followers of Christ. Their very presence is a

disturbing element to sin, and their joy is the most con-
tagious experience in the world.

There was an old Scotch woman who referred to a certain young man as one who would make a good minister.
She said, "He is a right harmless laddie." What an insult
this was to the ministry, and what a complete misunder-
standing of its demands! There are many characteristics
which are necessary for the Christian, but harmlessness is
not one of them. The Gospel appeals not to our lethargy,
but to our ambition. It is an answer to our human need to
be a part of a great adventure.

Answer to Discouragement

St. Paul was on his first missionary journey when he came
to Antioch in Pisidia. As was his custom, he went to the
Synagogue on the Sabbath and after the Scriptures had been
read, the elders invited Paul to speak. In the words of a
translation made by Ronald Knox, a Roman Catholic priest
of England, they said to him, "If you have any word of
encouragement for the people, let us hear it" (Acts 13:15).

A friend and I were talking about Christianity and he
remarked that it did not seem like comfort to him, but only
a disturbing discontent. As we talked about it, we came to
the conclusion that it is both a spur and a promise, or at
least it should be. If our religion is only comfort, certainly
something is wrong. But on the other hand, if it is not
encouraging, we have not reached its truth. Real Christianity holds these two things together so that out of its claim
on life, there comes its comfort.

We remember that some of the most bitter denunciations
were made by the Prophets and by Jesus. When they are
opening up the sin in society and the corruption in the
human heart, there is nothing very assuring in their words.
But it should not be forgotten that it was also a Prophet
who said, "Comfort ye, comfort ye my people, saith your

God" (Isaiah 40:1). Nor should we forget the gracious words of our Lord: "Come unto me, all ye that labor and are heavy laden, and I will give you rest" (Matthew 11:28). There seems to be a divine understanding of our needs in the Gospel. When we have grown discouraged with the seeming impossibility of ever finding a solution for the contemporary problem, it answers our discouragement.

It is a human tendency to look other places for encouragement first. We develop a great power of pretense and we learn to imagine brightness where there is only darkness. Our assurance may crack just a little but we pretend that all is well. A cloud not bigger than a man's hand appears on the horizon but we look at the expanse of sky that still has no cloud. Right to the end we hope we can muddle through.

There was an old woman who heard for the first time about the theory of evolution. It troubled her terribly as she listened to an exposition of its implications. Then she said, "God grant that it may not be true. But if it is true, God grant that not many people will hear about it." That is a human tendency. We will be optimistic for as long as possible. But when the time comes that we can no longer pretend, as it has come in our time, what shall we do then? Where shall we turn for hope?

We turn in vain to some word of encouragement from the economists. We thought at one time we had to worry only about the problem of overproduction. Now we are facing the problems of people starving to death because we cannot produce enough. The experts do not agree. Shall we make our conquered enemies strong enough to take care of themselves, or shall we keep them weak and pay for just enough food to keep them alive? Not only is the economic situation confused, but we doubt that even its solution would be the answer to the human problem.

Is there any hope from the political leaders? Haunted by

our dead dream of one world, we cannot find comfort for
our spirits in political manipulations and answers. How do
you contain a powerful, expanding country with an ideol-
ogy that is opposed to yours? How much can money really
accomplish? Is there any way to settle the minority problems and ease the racial hatreds? We may draw up the
blue prints and set up the political machinery, but without
the will for co-operation and the desire for peace, none of
these things will avail.

The militarists have a hard time convincing themselves
that they have any word of encouragement. There is no
defense against the weapons we have developed. Every
enemy you manage to kill, creates a hundred new ones. A
military victory is better than none at all, but not very
much better. Finally we begin to see that Jesus was speaking realistically when he said, "Put up again thy sword
into its place: for all they that take the sword shall perish
with the sword" (Matthew 26:52).

An advertisement appeared some time ago showing a
beautiful young queen standing outside her castle and
looking at her hand, which had a spot of blood on it. The
heading said, "Lady Macbeth needed a washing-machine."
Then it went on:

> Lady Macbeth was the original lather lady!
> She hated spots.
> In fact, it was a tell-tale spot of blood
>   that caused her downfall, according to
> Will Shakespeare, the Bard of Avon.
> All Lady Macbeth needed was some peroxide,
>   cold water and an electric washing machine
> To change her destiny.[1]

But we are no longer so sure that a few more gadgets will
change human destiny.

Our word of hope comes from the Gospel and it is the

[1] Quoted by Zeller, *op. cit.*, 39.

good news that God is like Jesus. In that affirmation we rest with confidence and trust. When Paul answered the request for a word of encouragement, he sketched the history of Israel and indicated the unmistakable signs of the presence of God there. Then he came to his great affirmation: God had broken into life in a climax to the whole process. Jesus Christ was a new power released in the world, and because of the Resurrection, the ultimate triumph of men was now assured. Ours is a word about God who is concerned with men and has bridged the gap between His ways and ours. We do not know that we shall win the next battle. The days ahead may be dark. But the outcome of the campaign is not in doubt.

A house-to-house canvasser stopped at an unpretentious cottage and was greeted by a weary mother. "Lady," he said, "I want to know how many there are in this family. How many children have you?" "Well," she said in a lei-surely fashion, "there is Johnny, and Mary and Charles and . . ." "No, no," interrupted the canvasser impatiently, "I don't want their names—just their number." And she answered indignantly, "They ain't got numbers. They all got names." The great word of encouragement the Gospel brings to men is that God knows their names—that the hairs of their head are numbered—that not even a sparrow falls, but that He knows and cares. For men lost in the wilderness of numbers with the night of fear falling upon them, the Gospel is their guide to personal dignity and en-couragement.

God's Grace

If we were face to face only with God's demands and with our own obvious inadequacies, there would be no answer to the human question. But there is that wonderful experience which we have summed up in a great phrase— the grace of God. It means that when we have exhausted every possibility, we find He has been waiting all the time to do for us what we cannot do for ourselves. We are trying to express the experience of the kindness of God's justice and of the wideness of His mercy.

Because we would rather assume we are up to dealing with the paradoxes of human experience, we try to solve our problems by ourselves. We keep trying to deal with things like prejudice and hatred as if they were intellectual matters instead of matters of the heart. Social workers do their best to minister to men by freeing them from their sense of guilt and arguing them into common sense. But nothing much happens. The world, as Luther said, is like a drunken peasant, and when you try to put him on his horse, he falls off on the other side. It is too bad that we cannot accept God's grace until we are at the edge of things. When we know at last only a miracle can save us, He gives us the miracle of His grace.

Men who are lost always assume that what they need is a leader. Yet the more they cry for such a man, the harder he is to find. At last, they turn to anyone who will boast the most and promise the most. They get the kind of leader who embodies their own weaknesses and leads them a little faster toward that dark future which they dread. But when men have been captured by Christianity, each man knows he ought to be great enough to lead. He knows then that salvation is not of men but of God's spirit moving among men.

Sometimes we seem to be cursed with mediocre leadership, but we get the kind of leadership we deserve. It is the faith of the people that produces the leader and the mediocre man is the result of mediocre living. Christianity has this sense of our unity and our interdependability. That is what Paul was saying when he talked about all of us being one body. We are all lost or we are all saved. It is not a brilliant individual who can lift the load of inertia. It is the grace of God touching the spirits of His children.

Men are always hoping for some external answer to this sense of directionless drifting. Science has been regarded as an answer for as long as possible, but science will not assume the responsibility of providing direction. It has prided itself on its objectivity, which means an absolute neutrality when it comes to weighing values or deciding which turning we ought to take. It can surround us with wonders and amusements, but it cannot help us find the way.

A secular educational system does not know how to deal with this problem because it is mostly a matter of teaching facts. We have spent considerable money for our educational enterprise. Most towns can be proud of their physical plants. In many an American city the most attractive buildings are school buildings. We have built gymnasiums and swimming pools. We have timidly experimented with what we have termed "character education." But we do not know about the education of the spirit. Can it be that without spiritual forces at work, the will cannot be educated? Yes, and we can find no answer until we assume the willingness of God's grace to do for us what nothing else is able to do.

The general panaceas never succeed in obtaining more than temporary and partial results. For a time, they seem to be the answer and we are always saluting a new dawn that is about to arrive. Men lose themselves in some reform program and give it the best of their energies. Or political parties challenge the interest of well-meaning people with their promise of a better world. But there are too many gaps left in all such programs. Something has to work on each human heart in the way that it particularly needs. There is no sense in talking about peace in the world until men can know peace in their hearts. It is this inner quality of men's lives that constitutes the problem and the answer has to be God's saving grace.

The perversity of human nature is nowhere more apparent than in the Crucifixion of Jesus. As Harold Phillips said, two men were crucified because they were too bad and one man was crucified because he was too good. When we see the grace of God at work in a life, so often we are frightened by it. We take our refuge in human institutions and human plans. There is a kind of madness which drives us on the way to further hopelessness. To confess that we have no answer is such a blow to our human pretensions that we sometimes kill when the tension becomes unbearable.

But the Christian has gone through this and come out safely. He has discovered that there is strength in weakness and power comes to the humble. United to his brethren with bonds of love, he becomes to his generation a strong force in holding the world together. It is not that personally he is a stronger or a more noble character than his neighbor. It is only that God has filled his need by the gift of His grace.

The Glowing Heart

The answer of the Gospel is finally apparent in the joy it brings to human life. This is something that skeptics always stumble over when they seek to disprove the reality of the Christian experience. Why should men be happy in the midst of suffering? Why do men rejoice in tribulation for Jesus' sake? From whence comes the irrepressible sense of humor enjoyed by those who have overcome the world?

In the story of the walk to Emmaus, the two men who had failed to recognize that the stranger was Jesus, finally had their eyes opened to his identity. They say in effect that they should have known who he was because, "Was not our heart burning within us, while he spake to us in the way, while he opened to us the scriptures?" (Luke 24:32). The sign of his presence was an experience in the heart.

Paul found Christ finally not by argument nor by reason, but by an experience which affected all his life. Whatever reasoning he might follow in seeking to explain the meaning of Christ, back of it all there was that light and voice which came to him on the road to Damascus. In all his preaching and writing, the Apostle assumes that Christians will know the truth of Christ by a presence in their hearts. Not by argument but by an experience of joy, does Christ approach us.

The power of John Wesley was not released until he had an experience in the Aldersgate Street Chapel. There, when his "heart was strangely warmed," his uncertainty was removed and the painful burden was carried away. Then he began that task of bringing living faith to the confused and careless masses of England. It is this experience of inner assurance and joy that releases a man from the tension of his doubts. And it means power.

Nothing is ever the same after the gift of the glowing heart has been bestowed. All of nature takes on a new meaning and the setting sun is no longer just a round, shining object, but a choir of the heavenly host singing praises to God, as Blake described it. Music now contains all the unspeakable glories of the heavenly melodies. It is not that a portion of the mind has been enlightened, but that now a man lives in a new earth and he sees a new heaven.

I am impressed with the joy of Christians. No people have such simple and profound pleasures. Other humor may be bitter or cruel. Theirs is kind for it is born of faith. They know that at the heart of the universe there is the everlasting Yea. They have looked at the worst, but they have not fled from it. At last they have gone beyond the dark night of despair to see the first signs of the coming day. It is this childlikeness that is so disturbing to the worldly wise. How can men be happy in the midst of the obvious ruin all around them? But the answer can never be given completely. We do not know why, but to the extent that we belong to Christ, his joy fills our hearts through every experience.

Praise is a central part of our religious observance. The Psalms are written by men who know all the devastating experiences of life. The hymns of the Church are an integral part of every worship service for we can hardly imagine worshiping God without wanting to sing. It was said that when Oliver Cromwell was dying, his friends stood around his bedside weeping. Almost his last words were: "Is there no one here who will praise the Lord?" Remember Paul's shout of triumph over the grave.

There are many things we do not know and we cannot know. But we know enough to live by. For the Christian, life is never a matter of just holding on. It is the great adventure in which God's grace brings encouragement to us when we are in need, and makes our hearts glow with an unspeakable joy. The Christian mind has found the answer!

XV

THE FINAL TRIUMPH

> *"The last enemy that shall be abolished is death."*
>
> I CORINTHIANS 15:26

H. L. Mencken said he had no desire for immortality and then went on to justify himself by declaring that belief in immortality issues from "the puerile egos of inferior men." John Haynes Holmes referring to this statement, listed a few of the "inferior men" who believed in immortality. The list included Socrates, Plato, Cicero, Seneca, Descartes, Spinoza, Kant, Goethe, Fiske, Edington, Lodge.[1] I would have included Jesus in the list.

We could hardly find a better example of the modern attitude toward fundamental issues than this. We have lost the horizon of eternity and in our blindness we say foolish things which sound sophisticated, but prove to be stupid when they are analyzed. To compare the little men of doubt with the big men of faith, is to see a contrast so marked that the cynics shrink from its implications. Doubt withers a personality. There is something about faith that is like the sun—it makes things grow. The modern mood is the product of the chilly atmosphere of denial. We grope in that darkness.

We are afraid life is futile. This is not something one could prove, but I think that underlying the conversation of many people, there is the feeling we are engaged in a project that does not really matter. War comes to a generation like this as a sort of relief, which is a terrible thing to say. But war for the time being dissipates the doubts we have as to the importance of our lives. We would like to be convinced of the importance of living, but when we measure it by length only, we cannot believe it is too important.

There is a feeling of personal insignificance. Many a man is a victim of what has become a popular cliché, an inferiority complex. Back of the nationalistic boastings and the hysteria of racial arrogance, there is a mad attempt to compensate for personal smallness. If we cannot feel significant in ourselves, then we will associate with a group and prove our superiority by persecuting a weaker group. Back of much of our rudeness and our hardness, there is the sense of personal inadequacy.

We have a feeling of insecurity. It is true, of course, that

[1] Holmes, *The Affirmation of Immortality*, Macmillan, 1947.

this world is never a safe place. There is a kind of security which we ought not to have and which we cannot have. This contemporary feeling, however, is something different. It is like being afloat in a sieve instead of a boat. A crew is aware always that it is the boat against the sea and they know the hurricane is dangerous. But when a man must bail every moment even in the calm sea, the contest is a fiasco. It means nothing. We must feel at least the significance of our striving.

There has been reborn in our time a new realization of the power of evil and the tragic implications of human life. Among the effects of a soldier killed in the South Pacific, there was found a notebook in which he had written:

> This is the time for new revelation. People don't think much about religion nowadays. But we need a voice from on High, brother, and I don't mean maybe. This thing has got out of human ability to run. I'm no religious fanatic. But we are in a situation where something better than human brains has got to give us advice.[2]

Not everyone looks for a voice from on high, but great numbers of people know that things are out of hand.

It is the lack of a standard or authority that deepens our despair. We have worshiped at the shrine of relativism for so long that we do not know where to turn when we need an absolute. It is no longer enough to take things as they come. We are in need of something that is the same yesterday, today, and forever. We have left the decision to the crew instead of to the captain, but in the time of our greatest need, the crew debates while the ship drifts toward the rocks. If only we had a captain aboard who would give the command that would save us!

Stephen Vincent Benét wrote these lines and entitled them significantly, "Thirty-five":

[2] Willard, *The Leathernecks Come Through*, Revell, 1944, 9.

> The sun was hot, the day was bright,
> And all July was overhead.
> I heard the locust first that night.
> "Six weeks till frost," it said.[3]

Those of us who are thirty-five or over will understand what
this means. Those who are under that venerable age, may
need a word of explanation. Benét was saying that until we
are thirty-five years of age, death is unreal so far as it con-
cerns us personally. Other people may die and do die. Our
fathers died, but we cannot believe we will ever die. When
we are halfway along through life, however, it comes to us
suddenly that the sands are running out. The second half is
always shorter than the first half and like a cold wind,
the thought strikes us that even as other men, we too, shall
die. There is also the fear that our civilization may be even
nearer death than we are personally.

The Book of Ecclesiastes is an expression of our mood.
It was written in a time of prosperity but also a time of
satiation. This is its word:

> I communed with mine own heart, saying, Lo, I have
> gotten me great wisdom above all that were before me in
> Jerusalem; yea, my heart hath had great experience of
> wisdom and knowledge. And I applied my heart to know
> wisdom, and to know madness and folly: I perceived that
> this also was a striving after wind. For in much wisdom is
> much grief; and he that increaseth knowledge increaseth
> sorrow.   ECCLESIASTES 1:16-18

This is life that has no answer to annihilation. The closing
in of the years is like the gradual closing in upon us of the
walls of our room. We cannot long be unconscious of it in
spite of all our efforts to think of other things.

H. G. Wells who had known periods of optimism came to
the close of his life with the most hopeless feeling. He was
convinced that the human experiment was at an end. Said
he:

[3] Copyright, 1942, by Rosemary Carr Benét.

Our world is like a convoy lost in the darkness of an unknown, rocky coast, with pirates in the chartroom and savages
clambering up the sides of the ship to plunder and do evil
as the whim may take them. Mind near exhaustion still makes
its final futile movement toward that way out or around or
through the impasse. . . . The writer is convinced that there
is no way out or around or through the impasse. It is the end.[4]

A Disturbing Voice

The strange thing about us, however, is that we cannot
adjust ourselves to this feeling of despair. This is the amazing
contradiction of human life. If we knew that death was the
end and life had no eternal meaning, we could finally accept
it. The human mind is marvelous in its ability to adjust
itself to the inevitable. Every man has had examples of that
in his own life. He has thought that if he had to face a certain tragedy, he could not endure it. But when it has come,
he has faced it and endured. When a blow to our best hopes
falls, we are first of all numb with anguish. Then gradually
we begin to stir again and time begins its healing work.
The day comes when we adjust ourselves to the death of
those seeming irreplaceable hopes, and we go on.

Yet we cannot do this when the hope of immortality is
gone. We may want to do it because it would solve the unbearable tension. Yet as Berdyaev has said in *The Destiny
of Man*, to disbelieve immortality is suspicious because it is
so comforting. It represents an attempt to find a way out
that is too simple. It is possible for a short time only, for
negative spirits. Robert Browning saw the difficulty of the
skeptic:

Just when we are safest, there's a sunset-touch,
A fancy from a flower-bell, some one's death,
A chorus-ending from Euripides—
And that's enough for fifty hopes and fears

[4] Quoted by Phillips, *In the Light of the Cross,* Abingdon-Cokesbury,
1947, 125.

As old and new at once as nature's self,
To rap and knock and enter in our soul,
Take hands and dance there, a fantastic ring,
Round the ancient idol, on his base again—
The grand Perhaps.[5]

The human situation is like a man who has left his career, his family and his friends to become a beachcomber on some far-off South Pacific island. He tries to forget his past and be satisfied to live out his remaining years as a derelict. He justifies his retreat from society, and his denial of responsibility. He does everything to lose the memory of yesterday and he tries to kill any hope of tomorrow. But something keeps reminding him of what he ought to be. He cannot forget his education and his gifts. He cannot justify his retreat. He has solved nothing actually, because now he knows an unhappiness deeper than ever.

This, I think, is the human dilemma. We will not find faith and we cannot be content with doubt. We are not willing to seek God as if we had to find Him, but we cannot sell our souls to the devil and be glad about it. Without a belief in the life everlasting, we are like men trying to build a bridge resting on one pillar.

Our need, if we are to live on a street called "Here" and in a city named "Now," is to build a fence around us that will keep eternity from breaking in. But we have not learned how to construct such a fence. We begin to think of personal relations and the first thing we know, we are thinking of God. We feel a sense of duty and yield to it. The next thing, we are asking why we should feel that sense of duty and we are driven to God's moral law. Even the most simple questions have a way of leading us out beyond our depth. It appears finally that being what we are, we shall never be able to build an eternity-proof defense.

Men behind the barbed wire of prison camps develop

5 Browning, "Bishop Blougram's Apology."

"barbed-wire sickness." It is nothing that can be treated by
a physician, for there are no physical symptoms. It is a
thing of the mind and of the spirit. It is something that
affects men who are confined for too long a time. There is
that same sickness that takes hold of human spirits when the
boundaries of this world are accepted as ultimate. Men get
sick because the temporal is not their natural habitat. They
were made for more distant horizons and longer views.

Men do not always believe in immortality because they
desire it. I have never been able to feel that the doctrine of
immortality is a product of shallow minds and romantic
spirits. Quite the opposite seems to me to be the truth.
Heroic attempts have been made to find substitutes for eternity and we have used all our ingenuity to provide enough
interesting things in this life to make the next one unimportant. We have defied man and knelt at the shrine of
science. Why do these attempts always fail? It is because after
a little time has passed and the novelty has worn off we cannot keep eternity from revealing the tawdriness of our
substitutes and trinkets.

This Life as an End

The attempt to build an earthly paradise has been a noble
one and for a time it was an acceptable one for many men.
The conquest of disease made rapid strides and it was con-
fidently expected that a time would arrive when most of the
pain and suffering of life could be eliminated. Life was getting longer, and perhaps one day in the future we might
expect to live twice as long as men live now. This was not
too encouraging for those who were about to die, but at
least it was a goal that promised better things for future
generations. Today, in contrast, we sit waiting for the first
diabolical use of germs to destroy life wholesale, and it is a
picture more horrible than we have ever considered. Now

we wonder if a few more years would make any appreciable difference in our existence anyway.

All of these things were proposed on the supposition that life is quantity and not quality. If we had enough things and a few more years, then we hoped to be satisfied with this world as the end of all. But the human spirit is not satisfied with just quantity. Life is a kind of experience and not a number of them. Men sometimes live longer and more profoundly in five minutes than they do at other times in five years. It is the inability of the world to provide the kind of experiences we hunger for that made this aim too small.

Count Hermann Keyserling once remarked that the greatest American superstition is belief in facts. If we can state our knowledge in a series of precise descriptions, we assume we have achieved truth. But who is to determine what a fact is? Well, a fact is what anybody can see and what can be proved. Be careful! You cannot live one day in this world on that basis. I cannot take one step forward without believing things I cannot prove and trusting people I do not even know. We try our best to live factually but it will not work. The facts are never enough. Man does not live by facts alone.

We are told that we must accept the fact that we will die. So we must. Then we are told that we must accept the fact that death is the end of us. Who said so? A materialist said so. But he began with a philosophy that cannot be proved and must be taken on faith. Why should I be asked to believe something he cannot prove? Besides, there is a great body of testimony to the effect that death is not the end of us. Says the materialist, "They cannot prove it." No, they cannot prove it and this, too, must be a matter of faith. It is never a choice between faith and facts. I must choose the faith that answers the most questions and fits best my experience. It will be the part of wisdom to observe what

kind of fruit is produced by any particular faith. The final
test is its effect on persons. Does it enlarge life?

Paul says death is a great enemy, which is to say it is a
great evil. It is the symbol of the incomprehensibility of the
world. If personality is the supreme thing, then it is a shabby
way to treat the supreme production. Every human relationship becomes a trap for misery and final defeat, if death
is final. So much of the dignity of life becomes triviality
and vanity, if death has the last word. We cannot escape
this feeling of defeat for any length of time. Life might
otherwise make sense if death was not a denial of any glim-
mer of purpose.

Now one of the things that seems to be true of all life
is its power to produce what the environment demands.
What we need, we develop, and through the years there is
going on a constant process of adaptation to our surround-
ings. Animals develop what they need to live where they are
supposed to live. On this basis, how do we explain the spiritual life of man?

There is such a wide variation between the mind and the
body. There seems to be no balance here that will help
man be at peace with himself. On the contrary, there is a
constant tension. While the body grows weak, the spirit
may grow strong. The spiritual side of a man's life so often
reaches its zenith at the very time his body is growing
weaker. Why should it be if this world is all there is?

In the words of James Martineau, we seem to be over-
provided for if life is to be terminated by death. We do not
need this spiritual equipment for our overnight stay on the
earth. As a matter of fact, it is often the very thing that
makes it difficult to be at ease on our journey. It would
seem as if man is equipped for something beyond this world
and that his experience here is a preparation for something
even greater. Martineau went on to say that "we do not believe immortality because we have proved it, but we for-

ever try to prove it because we believe it." This is an important distinction. It is our spiritual nature that cannot settle down here as if this were our home. We are driven to seek reasons for the mind because the spirit is already convinced that there is more to come. The root of the matter is not in any philosophy but in the nature of man himself. We are as travelers on their way to a destination beyond the stars. We always lay our heads in a foreign land when the day is done.

Much criticism has been made of the eternal viewpoint as an excuse for social unconcern. We are familiar with the revolt against a promise of "pie in the sky." A very imposing case has been built against religious institutions which fail to act in the interests of social justice now. They have been portrayed as contemplating a time after death when each man will get his just deserts. The supposition is that the other world is an enemy of this world. Those critics believe that if we could only destroy the whole idea of the other world, then men would spend their time and energy reforming this one. It is a convincing idea until you follow the implications of the argument.

No one wants to justify the appeasement of evil in the name of the comfortable doctrine that assures us everything will be set right after death. But the falsity of the "this world only" point of view is shown by the fact that the struggle for justice here is not intensified by denying immortality. The only way to promote justice is to ground it in the faith that there is something owing to creatures who are ends in themselves. But when the humanist tries to make that assumption, he finds himself cut off from any logical support. If men are here for a short time only, does it make any final difference how they treat one another? Does the treatment of men seem to be of eternal significance if men are not eternal creatures? The foundation of social concern is a religious assumption about the nature of men.

Codes of ethics or moral pronouncements all stand or fall on their answer to the question, Why? If we say a man must be free, again the question to be faced is, Why? If a man is an automaton, is there any convincing reason why he should be free? Am I supposed to be just to cattle? I have a right to kill them for food? We say yes to that because cattle are of this world only. But if a man is regarded as of this world only, what sense does it make to talk about a vast distinction between my treatment of a man and my treatment of an animal?

The realization is finally driven home to us that to maintain what we would call decency in our society, we must treat men as creatures of eternity. Whenever a society forgets that, the most horrible things can be done to men. When men cease to believe in immortality, they cannot even make things work here. So if a man says it is inconsequential or at least secondary, whether he believes in immortality or not, he is wrong. It is a matter of first importance. The world has been going from bad to worse ever since it took its eyes off the next world. Instead of being a matter of interest to theology alone, this is a matter that ought to be the concern of any realistic person. This life here is not enough and cannot make sense. Men are such creatures that only when their eyes are beyond this world, can they live in this world. Men are so made that until they can believe the last enemy has been vanquished, which is death, they are only half alive.

The Victory

At the center of the Christian faith, there is the Resurrection of Jesus. Some moderns have objected to the amount of space in the New Testament devoted to the Easter story. Why not spend more time discussing the life and teachings of Jesus? they ask. Their assumption is that we are encouraged to spend too much time on what is secondary and we neglect the most important part of the Gospel. But such thinking is wrong. Those early Christians knew that the heart of their message was an announcement that the power of God had raised Christ from the dead. Admittedly, they did not know just what happened and some of their accounts seem confused. They could not find the precise words to express it and they fell back on symbolism to suggest their meanings. But the central truth of the experience they never doubted and they made it the center of their message.

Christians can never explain the Resurrection because it is the Resurrection that explains them. The rationalistic interpreters of Christianity can never find reasons convincing enough to be substituted for the Resurrection. Their logic always has a gap in it. The whole Christian movement demands the Resurrection in order to account for it. It is much more of a strain on our credulity to believe that the disciples were the victims of a hoax, than to believe that their Lord was raised from the dead. I am frank to confess that I do not know the details of what happened on the Third Day. But I have been driven by the inadequacy of all other explanations, to believe that the Gospel which I have been called to proclaim, is rooted in Jesus Christ's victory over death.

The New Testament writers grasped the central fact that what Jesus is stands for more than what he said. This is not to minimize the teachings and the ethical principles. But Paul was right when he talked about the Risen Christ rather than the Sermon on the Mount. For the Risen Christ was the key that men needed. There were many good teachers who were saying, and had said, some fine things. It has been pointed out by Jewish scholars that you can find a parallel for nearly everything that Jesus taught, either in the Old Testament or in the latter writings of their scholars. Much can be made of the fresh and convincing style of Jesus' teachings, of course. But the unique message of Christianity is that the hope men had for the persistence of their spirits after death, was wondrously confirmed in the Resurrection of Jesus.

At the Battle of Marston Moor, the Cavaliers and the Puritans were poised ready for action. Then just before the trumpets sounded, Oliver Cromwell came riding across the plain. At the sight of him, the Puritans set up a mighty, victorious shout as if the battle were already won. This is what the Resurrection means to Christians. Much remains to be done and much sacrifice will still be demanded. But the battle will be won and the victory will be attained, for we see the Risen Christ.

Photographers learn that it makes a great deal of difference where the camera is placed. Most of us have taken pictures where the subject turned out to be all feet. This did not mean there was anything wrong with the feet, but only that from where we stood, we had thrown things out of focus. The Resurrection has become the point where we stand to see life in proportion. When we stand there, we see values in their right setting. That which is cheap looks cheap in the light of this reality. Things we have neglected because of our business with other matters, suddenly assume the importance of eternity. Things fall into place and life begins to make sense when it is interpreted in the light of the Resurrection experience. The terrible questions that haunt our minds find answers. It was no wonder the early Christians made this the center of their message. This is what the world had been waiting to hear. As Paul said after discussing the wonder of the eternal life,

> Wherefore, my beloved brethren, be ye steadfast, unmovable, always abounding in the work of the lord, forasmuch as ye know that your labor is not vain in the Lord.
> I CORINTHIANS 15:58

Christians have felt the certainty of the Resurrection because they themselves have been as men brought back from death. This is the note that runs all through the Pauline

Letters and to some extent it is discernible in all Christian writings. Christians have been raised from the death of sin. From the death of fear, they have been saved. To search for peace and receive it in more abundance than our imaginations would let us hope for, is like being raised from the dead.

Men who have known this experience have little doubt that He who brings them these gifts will also bring them victory over death. Some little girls were being told the story of Abraham and his sacrifice of Isaac. Everything went along very well and the teacher, with a dramatic touch, made it live. Suddenly as the story approached its climax, a nervous little girl burst out: "Oh please don't go on—the story is too terrible." But a second little girl spoke up at once saying, "Oh Mary, don't be so silly. This is one of God's stories and they always come right." Something of that is in the background of the Christian's thinking. He has experienced too many of God's stories which came out right in Christ, to believe that the greatest story of all will end in disaster.

To those who have been united through Christ, there is no separation. The continual presence of loved ones who have left us for a while, whispers the assurance that there is no death. My friend Dr. K. Morgan Edwards pointed out one of the most beautiful instances of this I know. He said that Arthur John Gossip, the famous Scotch preacher, lost his wife in the twenties. In a book he wrote in 1929, he surprised some of his friends by inscribing it: "To My Wife —My Daily Comrade Still." Then in 1945, twenty years after her death, he published another volume of sermons and he inscribed it: "To My Wife—Now a Long Time in the Father's House." Do you not see what this means? This is an experience that has already tested the promise of the Gospel and found it to be true.

We have forever. The passing days are not hastening us to our doom. They are leading us to the green pastures and the fellowship of the saints. When we begin to live in the light of this Christian assurance, we begin to understand the joy of the saints. There is nothing that is left untouched by it. All of our life takes on an eternal quality. Wilbur Cosby Bell, a great teacher of ministerial students, learned that he was about to die when he was in the midst of his best years. He said this:

> Tell the boys that I've grown surer of God every year of my life, and I've never been so sure as I am right now. I'm glad to find that I haven't the least shadow of shrinking or uncertainty . . . I've been preaching and teaching these things all my life, and I'm so much interested to find that all we've been believing and hoping is so.

The world wallows in its despair and lies limp in the bonds of its fatalism. The message for it is not just an urging to be better and to try harder. This is precisely what it cannot do. A moderate poetess says sweetly, that just the art of being kind is all the sad world needs. But this is just the art we cannot learn. This is our failure. There must come a message of the redemption of life by one who can bring us into the light of eternity. We want to come home again after the long years of wandering in the wasteland of humanism. We want God.

No argument will avail in this present hour and words will hardly succeed in cleansing our life of fear. Men must see the eternal light breaking through into their darkness. That means that it must come out of the lives and actions of men. Hugh Thomson Kerr tells of a little boy who had traveled in Europe and visited the cathedrals. He was asked one time to define a saint. There came to his mind at once the saints he had seen on the windows of the cathedrals and he said, "A saint is a person who lets the light come through." Then let us be saints! We are to let the light of our Risen Lord shine through us so that they who walk in darkness may see the light. For the last enemy has been abolished, even death.